ERRATA

p. 57, cat. 87
for *Miss Betty Stein* read *Miss Beatrice Stein*
("Miss Bea" of A.&P. 261)

p. 89, cat. 191
for *Farnsworth Museum* read *Jewett Arts Center*

Frontispiece. HOMME DESSINANT (Self-Portrait). 1935. Oil

jacques villon

master of graphic art (1875-1963)

published by clarke & way, inc., new york

museum of fine arts

boston

acknowledgements

America has always had a warm regard for the work of Jacques Villon, though it was not until 1950, when he was awarded the Grand Prix at the Carnegie International exhibition in Pittsburgh, that his reputation was established on this side of the Atlantic. The first of our countrymen to champion Villon was the American critic Walter Pach, a participant in the early parleys of the *Section d'Or* at Puteaux, who influenced Villon's inclusion in the New York Armory Show. In 1923, in a series of articles which appeared in *The Freeman* (expanded the following year in a book entitled "Masters of Modern Art"), Walter Pach wrote feelingly of Villon: "for it is he, I believe, who, more than anyone else, continues to express the indomitable spirit of adventure, the beautiful youth of the world's mind in the days before the war."

The Museum of Fine Arts, in collaboration with the Boston Public Library, takes pride in presenting the first major retrospective exhibition of Jacques Villon's graphic art since the splendid display of his prints at the Bibliothèque Nationale, Paris, in 1959, organized by Jean Vallery-Radot and Jean Adhémar. With the death of the artist on June 9, 1963, it now assumes the character of a posthumous tribute to seventy productive years of graphic excellence. The collective substance of Boston's print collections recommends this responsibility. In 1950 a member of the staff in the Print Room of the Boston Public Library, Mrs. Walter P. Robinson, was taken by Monsieur Pérussaux, collaborator in the catalogue raisonné of Villon's prints, to visit the artist in his studio. By chance, there resulted the opportunity of acquiring for the Library a collection en bloc of the artist's graphic work which Arthur Heintzelman, then Keeper of Prints, eagerly welcomed. Despite the unexpected death of Albert H. Wiggin, benefactor of the Public Library's Print Room, funds were made available for the purchase of this choice selection. The Museum is indebted to Milton Lord, Director of the Boston Public Library and Sinclair Hitchings, Keeper of Prints, for their willingness to share this rich collection in honor of the occasion.

To Jean Cassou, Conservateur en Chef du Musée National d'Art Moderne, Paris, we owe special indebtedness for the preface which he has graciously contributed as an inspiring tribute to the artist. Our appreciation also to Bernard Dorival, Conservateur, for arranging details relative to the loan of the drawing, *Soldats en Marche*.

To Madame Simone Frigerio we express our appreciation for her lucid introduction.

To William S. Lieberman, Curator of Drawings and Prints, Museum of Modern Art, New York, who organized in 1953 the first retrospective of Villon's prints in this country, our thanks for authorizing the loan of twelve prints. To George Heard Hamilton, Curator of the Collection Société Anonyme, and Egbert Haverkamp-Begemann, Curator of Drawings and Prints, Yale University Art Gallery; to Harold Joachim, Curator of Prints and Drawings, The Art Institute of Chicago; to Henry S. Francis, Curator of Paintings and Prints, and Leona Prasse, Associate Curator of Prints, Cleveland Museum of Art; to Mrs. Reginald H. Phelps, Director of the Farnsworth Museum, Wellesley College; to Agnes Mongan, Assistant Director and Curator of Drawings, and Ruth Magurn, Associate Curator of Prints, Fogg Art Museum; to Philip Hofer, Curator of Printing and Graphic Art, Harvard College Library; to Karl Kup, Curator of Prints, The New York Public Library; our gratitude for distinguished loans.

The following lenders have been generous in contributing from their private collections: Robert B. Appleton, Sidney Elliott Cohn, Richard Cox Cowell, Peter Deitsch, Mr. and Mrs. Joseph M. Edinburg, Mr. and Mrs. Samuel Glaser, Edward Powis Jones, R. G. Michel, Dr. and Mrs. Milton R. Sapirstein, Mrs. St. John Smith, Mr. and Mrs. Irving M. Sobin and Benjamin Sonnenberg.

The loan by the Galerie Louis Carré, Paris, of 12 prints and 24 drawings and water colors provides a vital supplement to the exhibition. Likewise, we acknowledge loans and generous assistance from the Peter Deitsch Gallery and R. M. Light & Co.

To Louis Carré personally, who has played a unique role in bringing Villon before the public, we are indebted, not only for the loan of the self-portrait in oil, *Homme dessinant*, but also for his unflagging interest and staunch support. Further obligation is due to Mademoiselle Chantal Maisonnier for compiling the biographical note, for tireless research, advice and copious correspondence.

To Mrs. St. John Smith and Mrs. John S. Reed of the Department of Prints and Drawings our special thanks for undertaking the compiling of the catalogue section and contingent duties; to Carl Zahn, Designer for the Museum, appreciation for the infinite detail and patience involved in designing the catalogue, as well as to David B. Little, Secretary and Registrar and his staff for arranging loans and insurance. To Harold Hugo and his staff of Meriden Gravure Company, our thanks for faithful service. Also, we wish to acknowledge the assistance of Mrs. Yolande Le Witter for advice in details of translation. Finally and not least, our thanks to Perry T. Rathbone, Director, and to Henry P. Rossiter, Curator of Prints and Drawings, for interest and support.

PETER A. WICK

70. HOMME LISANT. 1929. Etching

preface: jacques villon

Dès son arrivée à Paris et durant les premières années de sa jeunesse difficile, Villon dessina des caricatures pour les petits journaux anarchisants de l'époque. Arrêtons-nous sur ces ouvrages de début: une chose m'y frappe, c'est que le trait y apparaît moins comme un trait de dessinateur que comme un trait de graveur. Il est aigu et court, ne tend pas à dépasser la page, et celle-ci est exclusivement dominée par les fortes oppositions des noirs. On peut reconnaître en ces dessins le caractère essentiel de l'artiste: c'est un graveur.

Il s'exerce à la gravure et y triomphe avant que de se trouver comme peintre. C'est à la gravure qu'il recourt quand le presse la peine de vivre. Par exemple à son retour de la guerre de 14 et surtout pendant les années 25 où il exécute, d'après des peintures des contemporains, toutes ces planches en couleurs qui sont aujourd'hui à la Chalcographie du Louvre. Et toujours cet esprit minutieux et concerté, ce merveilleux ouvrier se passionnera, s'y perfectionnant sans cesse, pour les métiers du noir et du blanc, pour tout ce grand art de la gravure que les plus grands, Rembrandt, Goya, ont porté au sublime. Bref de par sa nature, en sa profondeur congénitale, voilà ce qu'il est, notre Villon: un graveur. Et lorsque les conditions de sa vie le poussent à une expression immédiate, cette expression c'est la gravure. Par vocation comme par nécessité, il doit exceller dans les arts graphiques et y devenir l'un des plus admirables maîtres de tous les temps.

Ceci ne fait que plus exactement mesurer l'étendue de son génie. Car ce graveur né, et si parfait, est devenu aussi, par une autre voie, plus lente, mais, à son terme, non moins souveraine, un admirable peintre. Ce maître du noir et blanc est devenu un maître de la couleur, et, là aussi, un des meilleurs de tous les temps. C'est un des plus savants coloristes qui aient jamais été, en même temps que l'un des plus prestigieux, séduisants, adorables. Comme quoi on peut contempler, en Jacques Villon, un génie fait pour un métier sévère, parti pour une carrière de progrès artisanal, de calcul, de patience et en même temps accomplissant une oeuvre, la plus délectable, de musicien, de magicien, d'enchanteur. Ce double itinéraire étonne car il a quelque chose d'exceptionnel et de miraculeux. Mais aussi il nous inspire un sentiment de tendre et fervente gratitude quand nous évoquons celui qui l'a réalisé, le cher Villon, de qui la grandeur, comme celle des saints, était faite de vertus humbles: pureté, simplicité.

JEAN CASSOU
Conservateur en Chef
Musée National d'Art Moderne

December, 1963

From his arrival in Paris and during the first years of his trying youth Villon drew caricatures for the little satirical journals of the period. Let us pause over these early works: one thing strikes me about them, namely that the line appears less like the stroke of a draughtsman than the stroke of an engraver. It is sharp and short, tending not to go beyond the page which is exclusively dominated by the strong oppositions of darks. One may recognize in these drawings the essential character of the artist: that of an engraver.

He practices engraving and triumphs in it before finding himself as a painter. It is to engraving that he resorts when he feels the pinch of need: for example, on his return from the War of 1914 and especially during the late twenties when he executed all those color plates after contemporary painters which are now in the Chalcographie du Louvre. And always this meticulous and deliberate spirit, this marvelous craftsman will be impassioned, ceaselessly perfecting himself in the métier of black and white, in all this great art of printmaking that the greatest – Rembrandt, Goya – have carried to the sublime. Concise by nature and in his inherited profundity, there he is, our Villon, an engraver. And when the conditions of his life impel him to an immediate expression, this expression is engraving. By vocation as by necessity, he must excel in the graphic arts and become thereby one of the most admirable masters of all time.

One thing makes us measure more exactly the extent of his genius. This born engraver, and so perfect, became also, by another path, gradual but ultimately no less sovereign, an admirable painter. This master of black and white became a master of color, and here also one of the best of all time. He is one of the most knowing colorists who ever lived, at the same time one of the most captivating, alluring, exquisite. Let us contemplate in Jacques Villon a genius made for an exacting craft, embarked on a career of artisan development, arithmetical, patient, and at the same time accomplishing a most delightful oeuvre, musical, magical, enchanting. This twofold itinerary astonishes, for it has something of the exceptional and miraculous. But also it inspires in us a sentiment of tender and fervent gratitude when we evoke the one who has achieved it, the Villon dear to us, whose grandeur, like that of the saints, was framed of humble virtues: purity, simplicity.

(*Translated from the French*)

1. PORTRAIT DE SON PERE. 1891. Etching

2. PORTRAIT DU PEINTRE-GRAVEUR, EMILE NICOLLE. 1891. Etching

Il construit un tableau
un épi, une rose
un visage, un sein nu

(Paul Eluard, *Jacques Villon ou l'Art Glorieux*)

Jacques Villon is no more. . . . His last paintings are full of such radiant youth that they make us forget that the first graphic works by Villon go back to the sources of the twentieth century. The exhibition organized by the Boston Museum of Fine Arts has the force of an historic testimony. Jacques Villon's drawings and engravings form an essential part of his work; in the light of them, the artist's line of pictorial development becomes clear, and it can be traced with accuracy, as is fitting, in the context of the great artistic movements of the last fifty years, that of Cubism in particular.

Jacques Villon's real name was Gaston Duchamp. He was born in 1875 at Damville, in the Department of the Eure, in a well-to-do family all of whose sons became famous. Gaston, the eldest, took the pseudonym of Villon, no doubt because he loved the satirical spirit of the first French popular poet, the Villon of the fifteenth century. Even in childhood, Jacques Villon showed an extraordinary gift for draughtsmanship; he was very early initiated into the etching technique by his maternal grandfather, Émile Nicolle, a painter-engraver of repute, to whose home he used to go on Sundays while a boarder at the Lycée Corneille in Rouen. Villon himself has recounted how, at the age of sixteen, he succeeded in making his first etching, a profile portrait of his father. He was generally, moreover, to show a preference for the etching technique, rather than the engraver's burin. At the close of the last century, learning to draw was the first stage in any painter's education. No artist could afford to dispense with an apprenticeship he shared with the humblest artisan, and the secrets of the craft were handed on from generation to generation.

Determined to give up the career of law which had been chosen for him, Jacques Villon came to Paris, where his brother Raymond, the future Cubist sculptor, Duchamp-Villon, was living. He devoted himself to etching and painting, and attended the Cormon studio, which had a great reputation at the time. Gauguin and Van Gogh, among others, had been there before him. Villon had already done some drawings for illustrated papers while at school in Rouen. In Paris, he continued until 1910 to draw for *Le Rire*, *Gil Blas*, and in particular for the *Courrier Français*, while at the same time doing lithographs and colour engravings for the publisher Sagot.

About 1900 satirical drawing was a flourishing art form. Following on Goya, Gavarni, Daumier, and under the influence of the Japanese prints set in fashion by Edmond de Goncourt, the modern style in drawing was about to see the light of day, thanks to Toulouse-Lautrec, Degas, Seurat and the Nabis. To these draughtsmen of renown must be added Jacques Villon. It is an astonishing discovery today that in his youth Villon, like Lautrec, Bonnard, Vuillard, did posters and programme illustrations for cafés and music halls.

Even Kupka and Juan Gris, friends of Villon's, gave drawings to the *Assiette au Beurre*. Montmartre and the Moulin-Rouge, haunt of artists, provided Jacques Villon with themes which are a faithful reflection of this period which has been called "La Belle Epoque." An aquatint in colour done by Villon in 1903, *Les Cartes*, bold of subject and very freely composed, shows a clearly original feeling for painting.

At this time, Jacques Villon began to exhibit at the Salon d'Automne as a painter. In 1906, he went to live at Puteaux, on the outskirts of Paris, where he was to remain all his life, keeping the same studio until his death. This Puteaux studio soon became the rallying point for a group of artists, which included Villon's two brothers, Raymond and Marcel Duchamp (forerunner of Dada and "anti-painting"), their sister Suzanne, joined later by Albert Gleizes, and, after 1912, La Fresnaye, André Mare, Fernand Léger, Picabia, Metzinger, Severini, Boccioni, René-Jean, Paul Fort, Napoléon Roinard and the American painter-critic Walter Pach. Critics, André Salmon and Ribemont-Dessaignes among others, and poets, notably Apollinaire, took part in these animated gatherings where new ideas were played with, ambitious theories set up: Cubism was in the air, no less at Puteaux in Jacques Villon's group, than at the Bateau-Lavoir in Montmartre, where Braque and Picasso were working. The two nuclei of Cubism were independent of each other, but their researches were parallel. It is a superficial explanation of the advent of Cubism to treat this movement as a reaction against Impressionism. After Impressionism, it would never have been possible to go on painting in the same way as before.

In Paris, the evolution in art before 1914, which was to end in Cubism, first developed via drawing. This evolution was to become a revolution in the world of forms, and one can follow all its phases in the graphic art of Jacques Villon, from 1907 onwards. In an etching entitled *L'Aide Gracieuse* (1907) we feel that the importance given to the subject is waning, and that the artist is tackling problems of plasticity, of line and dominating volumes. Towards 1910 in *Bal du Moulin-Rouge* Villon is preoccupied with form and space relationships.

Villon admired Leonardo da Vinci; he had read his writings, and was to baptize his group at Puteaux "The Golden Section," in allusion to the famous "golden rule" of the ancients, who divided their sheet of drawing paper or their canvas into squares before painting, in order better to establish the proportions of their composition. The artistic application of mathematical rules had just been defined by Paul Valéry, who in 1895 had published his "Introduction to the Method of Leonardo da Vinci." All the concepts of Cubism and geometric abstract art are already to be found here. "From forms

139. MAIS QU'EST CE-QU'ON JOUAIT DONC DIMANCHE DERNIER ? 1899. Crayon and India ink

born of movements," he writes, "there is a transition to the movements which the forms are becoming, by means of a simple variation of duration . . . a stationary form may be replaced by a suitable speed in the periodic transfer of a thing (or an element) properly chosen." The progress in mechanical inventions at the opening of our century and certain audacious constructions (the Eiffel Tower) gave spectacular reality to the theories on movement which artists were beginning to apply.

Throughout his working life, in his graphic art as in his paintings, Villon persistently sought to express movement and space. Similar endeavours characterized the Futurists, but with Villon their inspiration is wholly different; they stem from a Cubist logic whose essence is entirely French, and which leads to formal abstraction. Even better than painting, graphic art, with its line modulations, its sober combinations of black and white, gave Villon scope for severely architectured compositions. Little by little, constructions which are less and less representational are reduced to stratified planes, even in the portraits. After his first etchings, Villon never ceased making portraits, at all periods, as could be seen from the exhibition put on last year at the Galerie Louis Carré, "La Figure dans l'oeuvre graphique de Jacques Villon." Comparing, for example, the stylistic approach in the portraits of *Renée* (drypoint, 1911, cat. 46) and in that of *Monsieur D. Lisant* (1913, cat. 55) it is interesting to measure the evolution which took place in two years. In other words, in 1913 Villon had almost finished his exploration of Cubism, but instead of allowing his art to become sterile through over-narrow theorizing, he was seeking the outlets which were to lead him, in the twenties, to abstraction (*Figure par Plans*, 1921, cat. 170). However, on the whole, his portraits retain a certain characterization; no detail is superfluous, but the essence is thrown into relief thanks to Villon's keenness of observation. The craftsman's skill remains in the service of a deeply moving human perceptivity. Villon endows his models with a spirituality and a dignity which are his own.

Villon's very extensive graphic experimentation was completed by his practice of colour printing. Between 1922 and 1930, difficult material conditions incited the artist to engrave aquatints in colour after contemporary paintings, by Van Gogh, Cézanne, Picasso, Matisse, etc. This work enriched his stock of technical knowledge, and gave him an opportunity of carrying further his pictorial researches on light. The luminosity of Villon's engravings is beyond comparison; this quality turns them into wall pieces, veritable pictures. This same luminosity radiates from his painting, which retains the glorious freshness of the colour aquatint. Jacques Villon's painting takes its style in part from his superlative graphic ex-

cellence; at the meeting place of Cubism and Abstraction, this is the art of a humanist whose originality lies in his having remained human. Etchings, drawings or paintings, the work of Jacques Villon forms a whole. He was in the vanguard when he exhibited for the first time in the United States in 1913 at the Armory Show, with Raymond Duchamp-Villon and Marcel Duchamp.

Half a century later a Villon exhibition is still in the mainstream of modern art. The poet François Villon bequeathed to literature a "Grand Testament;" we love to recite its lines. Jacques Villon, the painter, leaves to younger generations an artistic "testament" of which the time has come for us to realize the full impact.

SIMONE FRIGERIO

9. GUINGUETTE FLEURIE. 1899. Poster, color lithograph

22. MANEGE RUE CAULAINCOURT. 1904. Aquatint

master of graphic art

Poet of line, poet of light, poet of color, the spirit of the Master of Puteaux from the seclusion of his well-ordered atelier looks back over seventy years of creation – Jacques Villon, lately dean of French painter-engravers, modern master of our century. His superbly graphic line, whether mordant incision or silver filament or constructive prism of scored parallels, or the illusive, yet penetrable network screening the viewer from the viewed, all these linear variations carry an expressiveness, sensibility and technical control of the highest order. He had called himself *Cubiste Impressioniste* – though more recently stated that he had been more "impressionable" than "impressionist" – but the label still applies. Beyond the displacements and geometry of surface abstraction, within the spatial vacuum of interpenetrating atmosphere, of circulating, form-devouring light, the humanist image stands forever vibrant and serene.

There was no precocity in Villon's beginnings. Coming from a solid middle-class professional family, "the backbone of France," of a cultured background whose members domestically took to drawing, etching and modelling with the same natural diligence as a musical child scales the keyboard, Villon, then the 16-year-old *lycéen* Gaston Duchamp, made his first etching, a makeshift, academic profile portrait of his father, scarcely anticipating his later Cubist style. His grandfather, Emile Nicolle, a marine insurance broker in Rouen, had etched some architectural plates of sufficient merit to find their way into the Chalcographie du Louvre.

cat. 1

Four years later in Paris, once launched on a career of art in place of the law, he settled down on the rue Caulaincourt to a life full of the vigorous abandon and color of bohemian Montmartre. It was a natural consequence that he should absorb himself in the prevailing art currents of the day, and like his fellow-artists of the boulevards, Forain and Steinlen, frequent the cafés and bistros to sketch *la vie qui passe*. His first employment came from the *journaux amusants*, the illustrated newspapers for which he drew little croquis in the vernacular of the day, vignettes of the demimondaine, tradesmen, street life and social satire. These compact little studies were more simplified than their Impressionist prototypes. Brevity, discipline, the *trait cau-*

stique, chic silhouette, arabesque outline and oriental patterns of flat washes were the graphic vocabulary of these journals.

But the nineties were principally the golden age of color lithography wherein Toulouse-Lautrec was already the rage. His posters were plastered on every wall, along with those of Chéret, Bonnard and less famous contemporaries. Between 1895 and 1907 Villon himself produced more than 30 lithographs, mostly in color, and some 8 posters as well as several unpublished designs. Probably his first poster and largest was that of the *Guinguette Fleurie*, one of those smoky little garden cafés big enough to accommodate a potted aspidistra, where every night at 8:30 *la fleur des poètes chansonniers montmartrois* belted out noisy ballads to the accompaniment of accordion or piano. Next to the Moulin-Rouge this must have been one of the best advertised "spots" on Montmartre. But the most strikingly original of Villon's posters was *Le Grillon, American Bar* (1900) posed by the picturesque Monsieur Levey whose outrageous taste in dress recommended him as a fitting model for this spiralling twist of art nouveau.

cat. 9

This was a vital period for Villon during which his technical development, advancing more rapidly than his stylistic, was stimulated by the exciting currents around him. From 1899 until 1910 he produced some 175 etchings and aquatints quite independent of his illustrations for the satirical journals. In 1899 he executed his first color aquatints under the supervision of the master printer, Eugène Delâtre, who had schooled Mary Cassatt in the perfections of this technique. The *Danseuse Espagnole* is one of Villon's most charming successes, of which this exhibition shows not only the preparatory study in water color but two impressions of the print as well, one in dark brown and one in full color. The influence of Toulouse-Lautrec's poster of Jane Avril (1893) is apparent in the figure of the dancer. Back in his student days Villon had been impressed by a small exhibit of Lautrec's drawings in a color shop in Rouen. But in his print Villon's color is in subdued earth tones and the medium of aquatint produces a soft, diffused tone of a subtlety and elegance more in keeping with Degas.

cat. 3, 4, 141

Other color aquatints of great fascination followed.

In 1900 *Le Maquillage* shares gentle irony with color refinement. In 1902 *Premiers Beaux Jours* (Color Plate I) appeared, reminiscent of Manet and his heavenly blue, while *Manège, Rue Caulaincourt* of 1904, printed in a twilight tone of olive green, sheds a soft, nostalgic light over the tracery of Paris. About this time the upper crust elegancies of Helleu began to spread their perfumed scent along the boulevards, reflected in *La Parisienne* (1902) and *Le Potin* (1905), and in the degagé sweep of some of his later drypoint strokes. But Villon's instinct for formal design spared him the superficialities perpetuated by Louis Legrand, Félicien Rops and Willette. Bonnard seems to have touched Villon in the graphic tendency to flatten his planes. We discover this in the *Boudeuse* as early as 1900, but startlingly in *Les Cartes* (Color Plate II) of 1903 with its bold color pattern. On the other hand, in the delightful *Cake-Walk des Petites Filles* (1904) he draws closer to Mary Cassatt in the pure handling of color aquatint, while the background panel in orange seems almost proto-Matisse.

The movement toward Cubism on Villon's part was before 1913 an almost imperceptible evolution which began after his removal in 1906 to Puteaux, where he and his brothers began their private investigation of their formal theories. Graphically speaking, external evidences of Cubism were not immediately apparent in Villon's work except for a shift from color printing to black and white which itself became a substitute for color values. In 1908 there was a tendency for etching to give way to drypoint, resulting in more resonant contrasts, at the same time, a massing of solid areas of dark parallel strokes suspended in the white ether of the paper. Curiously, this is most apparent in the drypoint, *Jeune Femme au Piano*, which otherwise is a very conventional print. In 1909, however, the large drypoint of *Nu Debout, Bras en l'Air* reveals a definite advance in vision. This dramatic, highly expressive figure of a female nude with upraised arms is rendered with slashing strokes of velvety drypoint in a spatial vacuum. The figure is elongated, the forms simplified, the limbs still rounded but with knobby joints. A comparison with Braque's first Cubist etching of a female nude (1908) shows flatter, more angular planes with spotty little grids of short strokes like wire mesh, un-

related to the planes of the body, but with textural interest of its own. By contrast, the Villon nude is plastic with an ordered flow of line and torsional rhythm. No doubt, both nudes go back to Picasso's historic "Demoiselles d'Avignon," while Villon also shared his brother's interest in sculptural form.

In 1911 came the drypoint studies of *Renée*, the mulatto girl with a horrid, saturnine expression, but powerful portraits of great mass, the face enframed in a wooly skein of black hair, the head and body immensely round, yet with internal structure sharply angular.

Finally, we come to the critical point of Villon's development, the year 1913 when he suddenly fulminated a stream of ten brilliant Cubist portraits, all drypoints, which in scale and boldness of conception surpass in dramatic impact the pioneer efforts of analytical Cubism by Braque and Picasso. The most orderly of the compositions is the *Portrait d'Acteur* (*Felix Barré*). This half-length bust, three quarters to right, conforms to the pose of *Renée à Trois Quarts* and retains the same round volumes of face and body, but the inner planes of the figure under theatrical spotlight undergo a prismatic subdivision, alternating angular areas of light and hatched areas of dark. The figure without losing its identity merges with the background scenery of intersecting flats.

Monsieur D. Lisant is a portrait of his brother, Marcel Duchamp. Again the same pose is assumed as in *Portrait d'Acteur*. Except for the curved line of the skull the figure is composed of diagonals which radiate in astral rays from the center line of the figure, rays that fracture the form, exposing it to reflecting facets of light and dark. A curtain of thin vertical lines combs the surface. One is awed by this timeless and mysterious presence, as by the shade of some Renaissance prelate.

Yvonne D. de Profil, the artist's sister, is the largest of these polyhedral portraits, a freer composition than the others, forming a patchwork of interweaving planes. The solemn figure is seated in an armchair caught in the flicker of firelight. Rarely has one print through myriad variations of parallel strokes created such diversity of texture.

In many respects the tour de force of this whole series of Cubist drypoints is the still life, *La Table Servie*. Four drawings dated 1912 (published by Dora Vallier)

cat. 13
cat. 16
cat. 22
cat. 18
cat. 29
cat. 14
cat. 20
cat. 25
cat. 37
cat. 41
cat. 45, 46, 47
cat. 56
cat. 55
cat. 52
cat. 54

Color Plate I. PREMIERS BEAUX JOURS. 1902. Color aquatint

Color Plate II. LES CARTES. 1903. Color aquatint

41. NU DEBOUT, BRAS EN L'AIR. 1909. Drypoint

show the painstaking steps leading up to this intricate design. "When I make direct studies," Villon has said, "my drawings follow the inner movement, the inner line of the object which, like a tightrope, determines its unity. In other words, I make an analysis straight from nature, so that I may have the time to think it over." Laid out on a rectangular oak table with heavy spiral legs of provincial origin is a random arrangement of dinnerware. The table runs diagonally up to the right. One recognizes the Chianti bottle in the foreground, behind it a plate, and a bowl of fruit beyond. Water carafe, cruet, cups and saucers and other utensils strew the surface. The backs of two chairs are seen on the upper left. Foreshortened within the diagonal framework of the table top these round and cylindrical objects "decompose" into patches of light, seeming to writhe in a centrifugal action. Transparency and reflection augment this continuous interplay, yet the structural lines of force of the spatial envelope firmly contain the movement. It is at once still life and movement; *hommage à Cézanne*. The method in the progression of preparatory drawings is noted by Dora Vallier. The first on squared paper is a free outline sketch conveying the immediate visual contact with the objects. The second defines the broader planes, ignoring details. The third definitive drawing, with the addition of wash, models the details in space. The fourth, squared, in reverse of the other three but in the same direction as the print, superimposes the final sketch on the first. This fourth drawing conforms to the skeletal framework of the print before the addition of shading.

In 1914 his Cubist research came to a head with two
cat. 57 etchings, *Le Petit Equilibriste* and *Le Petit Atelier de*
cat. 58 *Mécanique*. For the first time the image is almost totally lost in abstraction through a system of tight parallel lines overlaying triangular planes which demarcate zones of shade from zones of light.

Five years elapsed, and after the Armistice Villon returned to the attack with surprisingly fresh vision. It is remarkable that while carrying the torch for Cubism beyond the synthetic stages of Braque and Picasso, he never allowed theoretical speculation to starve his sensibility or weaken the *élan vital*, the vital impulse of his art. "I had too much love for life to be a sectarian cubist," he said. It was consistent with his nature to

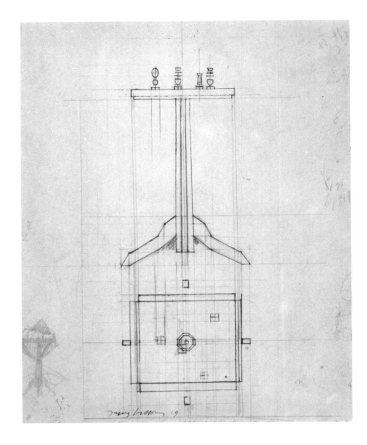

151. LA TABLE D'ECHECS. 1919. Pen

59. TABLE D'ECHECS. 1920. Etching

54. LA TABLE SERVIE. 1913. Drypoint

investigate other channels, while simultaneously re-studying the methods initiated in 1913.

cat. 59   The etching *Table d'Echecs* (1920), a theme identi-fied with the Duchamp family in life as in art, exempli-fies what he called *décomposition constructive*. It is an extension of the law of pyramids, the basis of his *Section d'Or* analysis. Villon defines this theory observing that "the ensemble of the oil is decomposed in colored pyramids marking the different points of view, points rather convergent, so that the pyramids can overlap one another to reconstruct the subject. This idea of the pyramid is borrowed from Leonardo da Vinci who in his treatise speaks of vision in pyramids. An object and the different parts of an object appear to us in pyramids, whose peak is in our eye and base in the object. There is even a second pyramid whose base is in our eye and point in the object." Throughout his career Villon plays upon this theme, in painting as in graphic art. The draw-
cat. 170   ing *Figure par Plans* (1921) is an example. Twenty years later he returns to it again in the color aquatint
cat. 114   *L'Univers* (Color Plate IV), a vivid, brilliant design. Actually, in all these compositions Villon has replaced his pyramids by planes, "superimposed planes which express volume."

cat. 60   In *Baudelaire avec Socle* (1920) Villon turned to a graphic solution of a plastic problem. This etching em-
cat. 191   bodies in splendid isolation the bust by Duchamp-Villon originally exhibited in the Armory Show. In this arrest-ing study of light modelling volume Villon has momen-tarily set aside his Cubist theories for a precise rendering of the object. With extraordinary technical skill the background is meticulously rendered in fine parallel lines of unprecedented delicacy, giving the vibrating textured effect of pandanus cloth.

The prints of 1921 were as few as they were small:
cat. 61   three etchings: *Noblesse*, *L'Oiseau* and *Le Cheval*. For an instant he seems to be approaching a phase of pure
cat. 168   abstraction. In the water-color study, *Noblesse*, a com-position related to the print, he treats an abstract theme abstractly. A sort of upright dignity and purity of color are the only clues to the subject. On the other hand, in
cat. 169   a tangible image like *Un Oiseau*, a free little water-color *première pensée*, the concept of the bird in flight is apparent. Certainly, Villon never lost sight of nature. "Abstraction," he said, "must have an attachment to

life. Total abstraction is not for me. I am too fond of life and of semblance."

In this period Villon became obsessed with an ex-amination of the racehorse. The painting of *The Jockey* in the Collection Société Anonyme at Yale University and the eight preliminary drawings from the same col-   cat. 157-164 lection have been published by George Heard Hamil-ton. In his words they "comprise one of the most authoritative documents for the reconstitution of the Cubist dialectic." Professor Hamilton describes the orderly progressive steps from visual appearance of horse and rider as seen in nature to their synthesis in geometric forms and colors on the surface of the can-vas. Measured drawings of the horse viewed first from above (No. 1), then in profile (No. 2), are followed by a   cat. 157, 158 drawing of the jockey sketched from above and in side view (No. 3). In the next drawing (No. 4) these pre-   cat. 159, 160 liminary studies are superimposed in pen, ink and water color, and the Cubist shapes take form through meas-ured analysis. The next stage (No. 5) is a tracing of the   cat. 161 previous, further reducing natural appearances to ele-ments of design. Then follows (No. 6) a mathematical   cat. 162 squaring into equal rectangles and the laying in of horse and rider in a tighter geometrical pattern divested of natural form. In the final drawings the process is quick-   cat. 163, 164 ened to its logical synthesis. Two further drawings in   cat. 166, 167 the exhibition relate to the Yale series, both of which appear to fit between Nos. 5 and 6, while the water color *Outsider* is a further variation on the theme   cat. 165 (Color Plate III).

Like all the French Cubists Villon had a passion for analysis of form which had its outlet in drawing. He never conceived of drawing as an end in itself, but as a logical step towards organizing a subject, of setting down the bones of his design, constructing the lines of force, establishing the rhythms observed in nature. "This rhythm I borrowed and am still borrowing from a rapid sketch, often a simple line, translating the principal movement of the subject, a veritable line of intuition of life passing through things, the spinal column of the picture."

If we liberate Villon's drawings strictly from the connoisseur's concept of a finished cabinet piece, we may discover significance and expression beneath the theoretical surface of his working drawings. Inevitably,

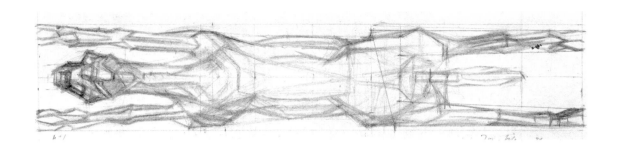

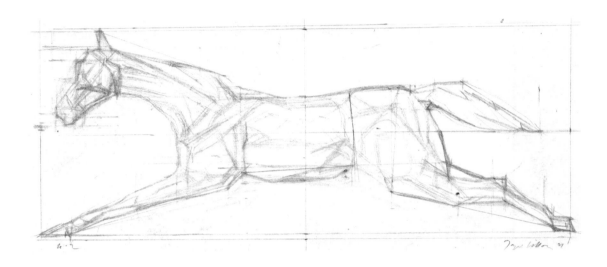

157. STUDY FOR THE JOCKEY, NO. 1. 1921. Pencil

158. STUDY FOR THE JOCKEY, NO. 2. 1921. Pencil

163. STUDY FOR THE JOCKEY, NO. 7. 1921. Pencil and pen

certain drawings have historic dimensions which out-weigh their immediate visual comprehension. Such a drawing is the early Cubist document *Soldats en Marche* from the Musée National d'Art Moderne in Paris. Dated 1912, the year of the first *Section d'Or* exhibition, it is a photograph of a plotted pencil draw-ing reworked in wash, preparatory for the painting of 1913. It records a troop march, an incident selected from direct experience and subjected on paper to a strict pictorial order. It is intricately constructed of delicate guidelines connecting points of demarcation. One can make out on the left the contours of a uni-formed soldier marching to the right, and soon the rhythmic progression of the marching troop is appar-ent. The diagonal lines of force are strengthened with wash. The drawing is incomplete without benefit of the clarifying color of the finished oil.

cat. 146

Another constructive drawing is *L'Athlète* after Duchamp-Villon's bronze, "Torse de Jeune Homme," exhibited at the Armory Show in 1913. The drawing, dated 1920, in black, red and blue pencil on tracing paper, seems to be a straightforward cubification of the original sculpture with a movement suggested more by the pose of the figure than by any inner dynamic.

cat. 156

Villon's work has been subjected to many miscon-ceptions over the years, which happily for the record he has dispelled in an elucidating statement published in the Paris weekly revue *Arts* in 1961 (April 26 – May 2):

Solitary work on a private road

"I have never very much liked theory. I have sub-mitted to the influence of a theory only at the moment of the advent of Cubism, which had not yet found its name. Picasso and Braque were the first to set out on this road. We were a group of friends, La Fresnaye, Gleizes, Picabia, Léger, Metzinger, my brothers and myself, and we were interested on our side in these in-vestigations. As for me I have not been cubist be-cause of doctrine, but because it suited me.

"My passage from one form of art to another, from expressive drawing to analytical Cubism took place a little before 1910. It was definitive. Several months after our group exhibitions in different galleries, the first Futurist exhibition in Paris took place in October, 1911. I had no knowledge of it at the time. Thus, I was rather surprised when I read articles by critics affirming that I had submitted to the influence of Futurism.

"This misunderstanding was born of a premature interpretation of certain of my paintings. Thus, *Soldats en Marche*, that had been identified with Futurism, has its origin in the croquis that I had made on manoeuvers in the course of a march during my military service. But it is one thing to be *in* motion, and quite another to ob-serve from the outside. Futurism decomposes move-ment, Cubism represents the object on every surface.

"In 1913 I had been working in a mechanic's shop in Asnières. That was another source of confusion. And then the war came; Cubism, Futurism, all the tenden-cies of that time had been put in error by the expansion of the event. In 1918 there survived no more than a vast movement, modern painting, which lasted up to the great crisis of 1930. But this mélange was a third cause of misunderstanding: when I took for a theme some racehorses, they began to speak of painting of move-ment. But I had never gone to the races! I had bought some little toy horses. I painted them from above, I cut them in slices in the manner of a geological cross-section.

"From 1930 to 1940 I painted absolutely alone; I was not very highly esteemed, but I was sure that as far as I was concerned people were wrong.

"It is perhaps this solitary work which has permitted me to appreciate all the young painters whose fervor I so admire. Today, continuing on my private road, I participate with serene joy in the flowering of what I already suspected when I painted back in 1931 my picture, *Naissance du futur.*"

From 1921 forward Villon's graphic output continued, not with the same preoccupation as before, since his contract with Bernheim-Jeune to engrave color repro-ductions after modern paintings, initiated as a financial necessity, consumed his energies almost exclusively. Nevertheless, up until 1930 when he was released from his contract, he made fourteen etchings in black and white, many of them capital works: one may cite *Sur les Rochers* (1927), a semi-abstract figure study in the open air, *Tête de Fillette* (1929), the haunting, terror-struck face of a young girl, and *Nature Morte aux Noix* (1929), a classic still life of fruit and nuts arranged

cat. 62

cat. 67, 68

cat. 71

146. SOLDATS EN MARCHE. 1912. Wash

156. L'ATHLETE DE DUCHAMP-VILLON. 1921. Pencil

cat. 72

within flattened Cubist planes. His prints of 1930 include *Les Haleurs* based on an earlier study of workmen hauling a cable, a reexamination of the rhythm of concerted physical movement in space. It is sometimes suggested that after 1930 he turned to painting at the expense of etching. In truth, his yearly output during the thirties averaged eight prints, a solid production indeed. And so he continued throughout the forties without relapse.

Monsieur Pérussaux has summarized the development of Villon's etching technique commencing with the thirties. From the powerful masses of the great Cubist drypoints of 1913 he advanced to a cooler, lower-keyed tonality, attaining a "serenity of structure," a greater refinement of line, utilizing an orderly system of parallel strokes crossing and crisscrossing the plate, diffusing the light through more balanced

cat. 77, 78, 173

cat. 93

contrasts. Still life is charmingly interpreted in such etchings as *Nature Morte au Perroquet* (1932) and *Le Baie du Petit Salon* (1938). The artist has stated: "I think that if my Cubism was not harsh it is because I have always preferred the human figure to still life. The human figure being alive, one can not, one dare not put him in chains." The human figure indeed assumes an increased importance in such portraits of great

cat. 80, 174, 175

temperament and sensibility as *Le Savant* (1933) in which the lessons of Rembrandt are interpreted with subtlety and spiritual penetration. The portrait of the

cat. 86

young American *Francis Steegmuller* (1935) is full of light and youthful optimism. The portrait of *Camille*

cat. 104

Renault (1945), the restaurateur of Puteaux, friend of the artist and responsible for a savory dish called *turbot Jacques Villon*, appears as a mountain of timeless humanity which a flood of light has failed to evaporate.

cat. 84
cat. 81
cat. 95

Landscape appears in such great plates as *Chevreuse* (1935), *Notre Dame de Vie* (1934) and *Les Trois Ordres* (1939). Particularly after his sojourn in the Midi in the forties, his landscape assumes an amplitude, a luminosity, effulgence. Throughout his mature years and into the final phase of the fifties there is an expansion and deepening of his style, a freedom of line and light opening the door to nature, achieving a universality in

cat. 103
cat. 112

such prints as *Globe céleste, Le Ciel* (1944) and *La Signature* (1951).

Villon has left a handsome oeuvre of illustrated books of which this exhibition has selected the outstanding examples, reflecting the artist's direct participation and the intimate collaboration of artist, printer and publisher. One might cite the lyrical *Cantique Spirituel* of Racine (1945), *Les Travaux et Les Jours* of Hesiod (1962), a pastoral elegy of magnitude with a delicate linear reticulation related to such late drawings as *La Ferme au Pigeonnier*. A minute little book, all too neglected, is Max Jacob's *À poèmes rompus* (1960) with glowing color aquatints, totally abstract expressionist. It is in such examples that his color is purest and most transcendant.

cat. 128
cat. 134

cat. 188
cat. 133

It is illuminating to quote in translation from the "Lettre de l'Artiste" in Jacques Lassaigne's *Eloge de Jacques Villon* (1955):

". . . I add my profession of faith as an engraver. I offer it to you in all simplicity:

"I love color. 'Colors' are my meat and drink.

"And yet it was not to color that I devoted my first years of apprenticeship, but to engraving, to lithography – in short, to prints – then to drawing.

"Why? My friend Jacques Lassaigne has just explained; because of the example set by my etcher-grandfather. But also – especially – because this graphism which seizes hold of an idea, encircles it in a noose, seemed better to suit my inquisitive turn of mind, that of the avid collector of gestures and attitudes, not merely like so many butterflies pinned on a cork, but as things in themselves, so to speak, synthesizing, concretizing a moment, so as to render it eternal, to illuminate it in a special, lasting way through the mysterious network of the copper which will entrust its secrets to the paper.

"Drawing is governed by the emotion it sets free, which corresponds to that which gave it birth.

"It may stray, find the road again, set out afresh; searching is its essence. Engraving, on the other hand, controls, it is precision par excellence. In order to master a difficult medium, the engraver must regulate everything in advance (at least in his mind's eye), look on his copper as one does a canvas, and divide it up harmoniously. An engraving is not, therefore, a simple drawing executed more or less rapidly on a copper plate.

Color Plate III. OUTSIDER. 1921. Water color

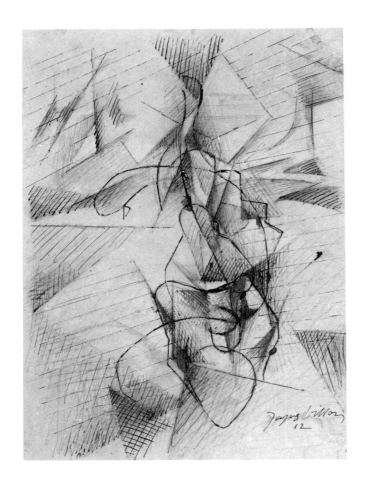 

147. L'EQUILIBRISTE. 1912. Pen

57. LE PETIT EQUILIBRISTE. 1914. Etching

176. NOTRE DAME DE VIE. 1934. Pencil

81. NOTRE DAME DE VIE. 1934. Etching

"Engraving discards the subtle craftsmanship of drawing, the subtlety of which is expressed by a thousand steps forward, a thousand back, as if, conducted by a thread, the artist had to find his way out of a labyrinth.

"In engraving, the subtleties of drawing are expressed, one might say, in depth. A tint expressed by a certain number of parallel lines, of strokes and counter-strokes, gives rise, when subjected to acid for periods of from two to twenty-five minutes, to a range of shades that one could express in drawing by repeated strokes of the pencil, or in ink, by a multitude of crossed lines.

"In simplifying the drawing, the engraver thus loses nothing of the thousand refinements of the spirit behind the draughtsman's hand. I am speaking, of course, of a painter's engraving.

"To the opposition between the ink's black and the paper's white is added the richness of the bitten line which is embodied in the paper, on which it overflows, diffused.

"If it were possible to ask Gulliver to enlarge a proof of one of our engravings, its lines would seem transformed into a fortified town.

"And this apparition in relief, evident, furrowing the paper, would double the interest of its metamorphosis feverishly awaited at the mouth of the hand-press."

Jacques Villon is a poet of precision. He approaches his drawing and engraving as an architect addresses his draughting board. He plots, he constructs, tectonic line, with T-square and triangle. The flow of line is in his hand, the cursive impulse in his spirit, and freely employed, but the straightedge is nearby to guide his structural line onto the paper, to erect the "spinal column." "My nature leads me to search for things well ordered," he declares. The reason Villon fails in his few attempts at the medium of black and white lithography is owing to the lack of resistance in this softer medium, its loss of incisive line. Villon even interests himself in certain problems of engineering, problems of light and ventilation in his graphic art that imparts its allure, its illusion, its surge of mystery.

Jacques Villon is cast in the classical French mold. "Art," he said, "is a distillation of emotional and physical origin in which intelligence wins over intuition." Yet, it is the balance of parallels in Villon, of oppositions, which give to his art depth and enrichment: painting versus engraving, color versus black and white, abstract versus concrete, doctrine versus sensibility, precision versus impulse. But line is the logic, the impulse and the vertebrae that crystallize the sensations of his art.

PETER A. WICK

85. MADELEINE. 1935. Etching and drypoint

biographical notes

prepared by chantal maisonnier

1875
Gaston Duchamp (the future Jacques Villon) born July 31 at Damville (Eure) in Normandy. His father was a notary; his mother the daughter of Emile Nicolle, etcher of architectural views. Gaston was eldest of seven children including brothers Raymond (the future Cubist sculptor Duchamp-Villon, born 1876), Marcel Duchamp (the future painter and Dadaist, born 1887), and sister Suzanne, also to become a painter and engraver.

Villon was a pupil at the *lycée* in Rouen.

1891
First two etchings: *Portrait de Mon Père* (A.&P.1) and *Portrait du Peintre-Graveur, Emile Nicolle* (A.&P.2).

1894
To Paris to study law, but soon shifted to career of painting and engraving. Took pseudonym of Jacques Villon. A brief attendance at the Atelier Cormon, boulevard de Clichy.

1894–1910
Drawings published in the weekly illustrated reviews, including *Le Rire*, *La Nouvelle Revue*, *L'Assiette au Beurre*, *Gil Blas* and especially *Le Courrier français*.

1895
First lithographs.

1898
After one year military service Villon installed himself in Montmartre, rue Caulaincourt.

1899
First color aquatints printed by Eugène Delâtre, rue Tourlaque. Some 165 of his prints published by Edmond Sagot, rue de Châteaudun, between 1899 and 1910.

1899–1906
Designed a number of posters of which some 8 were published as color lithographs.

1903
Exhibited at the Salon d'Automne where he exhibited yearly for the rest of his life; member of the committee until 1911.

1905
First exhibition at Galerie Legrip in Rouen with Duchamp-Villon.

1906
Moved to Puteaux-sur-Seine, Paris suburb, not far from his youngest brother Marcel Duchamp who lived in Neuilly; Villon joined by brother Duchamp-Villon.

1911
Changed publisher to Clovis Sagot, rue Lafitte.

1912
Organized in his atelier at Puteaux the artistic movement called *Section d'Or* inspired by Leonardo's "divine proportion" and Villon's personal theory of cubism based on the pyramid.
Exhibition, *Section d'Or*, Galerie la Boétie, 10-30 October, including Archipenko, Marcel Duchamp, Duchamp-Villon, Gleizes, Juan Gris, Marie Laurencin, Léger, André Lhote, Marcoussis, André Mare, Metzinger, Picabia, Jacques Villon, Dunoyer de Segonzac and La Fresnaye; accompanied by a symposium led by Guillaume Apollinaire.

1913
First cubist prints.
Villon exhibited 9 paintings in the New York Armory Show, where Marcel Duchamp exhibited *Nude Descending a Staircase*, and Duchamp-Villon 5 sculptures, including *Torse de Jeune Homme* and *Baudelaire*.

1914–1919
Mobilized for duration of World War I. In 21st Infantry Regiment until 1916, he fought in Champagne and Artois; afterwards attached to camouflage corps. Following demobilization he returned to studio in Puteaux.
Raymond Duchamp-Villon died in October 1918, a few days before Armistice.

1917
First exhibition of Society of Independent Artists, New York.

1919-1922
First abstract period.

1921-1930
To earn a living he engraved some 45 color aquatints for Bernheim-Jeune, reproducing paintings of modern masters, of which 29 have been published in restrike by the *Chalcographie du Louvre*. Engraved 34 plates for *Architecture* (1921), published under direction of André Mare.

1925
Last exhibition of *Section d'Or*, Galerie Vavin-Raspail, Paris.

1920-1934
First one-man shows of Villon in New York: *Société Anonyme* (1921); Brummer Gallery (1928) with 35 paintings; preface of both catalogues by Walter Pach. Exhibitions: Arts Club, Chicago (1934), 21 paintings and 10 prints, preface by Walter Pach.
Marie Harriman Gallery, New York (1934), 21 paintings.

1936
Trip to America.

JACQUES VILLON IN HIS ATELIER (1954). Photo courtesy Margo Friters-Drucker

1937	At World's Fair, Paris, Villon awarded two diplomas of honor, and one gold medal for painting and engraving.
1940-41	Before German occupation Villon left Paris, visited in Bernay with Madame Mare; then at the château La Brunié (Tarn) with Monsieur and Madame Marc Vène. Landscape influenced his art.
1944	Exhibition, *Jacques Villon*, Galerie Louis Carré, Paris.
1945	Exhibition, *Duchamp, Duchamp-Villon, Villon*, Yale University Art Gallery, preface by George Heard Hamilton.
1948	Exhibition, *Jacques Villon, 1945, 1946, 1947*, Galerie Louis Carré, Paris (29 paintings).
1949	Exhibitions: *Jacques Villon, Retrospektiv Udstilling*, Statens Museum for Kunst, Copenhagen (32 paintings); first retrospective by European museum. *Villon*, Louis Carré Gallery, New York (17 paintings), preface by Jerome Mellquist. *Jacques Villon-Lyonel Feininger*, Institute of Contemporary Art, Boston; Phillips Collection, Washington; Delaware Art Center, Wilmington (25 paintings, 19 drawings and prints), text by James Plaut and George Heard Hamilton. Awarded Grand Prix for engraving at exhibition in Lugano.
1950	Exhibition, Venice Biennale, Salle Jacques Villon (29 paintings), preface by Lionello Venturi. First Prize, Carnegie International, Pittsburgh.
1951	Retrospective, *Jacques Villon*, Musée National d'Art Moderne, Paris (85 paintings), preface by Jean Cassou. Exhibition, *Jacques Villon – Louis Moilliet*, Kunsthalle, Berne (53 paintings), preface by Jerome Mellquist.
1952	Exhibitions: *Villon*, Liège (37 paintings), preface by Frank Elgar. Lefevre Gallery, London (32 paintings), preface by Jerome Mellquist. Arts Club, Chicago (34 paintings). *Retrospektiv Udstallning Jacques Villon*, Svensk-Franska Konstgalleriet, Stockholm (42 paintings, 26 drawings and prints).
1953-54	Exhibitions: *Jacques Villon, His Graphic Art*, Museum

of Modern Art, New York (96 prints), preface by William S. Lieberman.
Jacques Villon, Oeuvre gravé, Galerie Louis Carré, Paris (59 prints), preface by Jean Adhémar.
Rose Fried Gallery, New York.

Villon awarded Commandeur de la Légion d'Honneur and Commandeur des Arts et des Lettres.

1955	Exhibitions: *Jacques Villon*, Musée Toulouse-Lautrec, Albi (48 paintings), essays by Edouard Julien and André Chastel. Lucien Goldschmidt, New York, publication of Virgil's *Bucolics* (25 color lithographs).

JACQUES VILLON AT HIS PRESS (1953). *Photo courtesy ART NEWS*

Grace Borgenicht Gallery, New York.
Jacques Villon, Peintures, Galerie Louis Carré, Paris (27 paintings).

1956   Exhibition, *Dessins de Jacques Villon*, Galerie Louis Carré, Paris, preface by Pierre Mazars.

Awarded Grand Prix, Venice Biennale (38 paintings), preface by Raymond Cogniat.

1957   Exhibitions: *Jacques Villon, Raymond Duchamp-Villon, Marcel Duchamp*, Guggenheim Museum, New York (27 paintings), preface by James Johnson Sweeney.
Hommage à Jacques Villon, Salon d'Automne, Paris (52 paintings), preface by Paule-Marie Grand.
Nasjonal Galleriet, Oslo (prints), preface by Jan Askeland.
Institut Français, Athens (prints and drawings).

1958   Grand Prix, World's Fair, Brussels.

1959   Exhibitions: *Jacques Villon, l'oeuvre gravé*, Bibliothèque Nationale, Paris (155 prints), preface by Julien Cain, text by Jean Vallery-Radot and Jean Adhémar.
Jacques Villon, Kunstnernes Hus, Oslo (80 paintings), prefaces by Alf-Jorgen and Henning Gran.

1960   Retrospective, *Jacques Villon, Måleri och Grafik, 1909–1959*, Moderna Museet, Stockholm (94 paintings, 58 prints), text by Carl Nordenfalk and K. G. Hultén.

1961   Exhibition, *Cent tableaux de Jacques Villon*, (60 drawings and prints), Galerie Charpentier, Paris, introduction by Raymond Nacenta, preface by Jean Tardieu.

Elected honorary member of the American Academy of Arts and Letters and of the National Institute of Arts and Letters.

1963   Exhibitions: *La Figure dans l'oeuvre graphique de Jacques Villon*, Galerie Louis Carré, Paris.
Jacques Villon (retrospective), Kunsthaus, Zurich (including 60 drawings and prints), preface by Eduard Hüttinger.

Villon, who had just been promoted Grand Officier de la Légion d'Honneur, died at his studio at Puteaux on June 9.

178. STUDY FOR LE GRAND DESSINATEUR (Self-Portrait). 1934. Pen and India ink

82. LE GRAND DESSINATEUR ASSIS (Self-Portrait). 1935. Etching and drypoint

selected bibliography

Books and Articles

Ashton, Doré. "Jacques Villon, Father of Modern Printmaking." *Art Digest*, vol. 27, no. 20, Sept. 1953, pp. 9ff.

Auberty, J., and C. Pérusseaux. *Jacques Villon, catalogue de son oeuvre gravé*. Paris, 1950.

Collection de Dr. Oscar Stern, prints, drawings and illustrated books by Villon. Hôtel Drouot sale, 23 Nov. 1962.

Crespelle, J.-P. *Villon*. Paris, 1958.

Dorival, Bernard. *Les étapes de la peinture française contemporaine*, vol. 2, *Le Fauvisme et le Cubisme*. Paris, 1949, pp. 309–317.

Eluard, P. and René-Jean. *Jacques Villon ou l'art glorieux*. Paris (Louis Carré), 1948.

Hamilton, George H. "The Dialectic of Later Cubism: Villon's Jockey." *Magazine of Art*, vol. 41, no. 7, Nov. 1948, pp. 268–272.

Lassaigne, Jacques. *Jacques Villon*. Paris (Beaune), 1950.

———— *Éloge de Jacques Villon*. Paris (Bruker), 1955.

Lieberman, William S. "Jacques Villon: His Graphic Art." Museum of Modern Art *Bulletin*, vol. XXI, no. 1, Fall 1953.

Mellquist, Jerome. "Jacques Villon." *L'Oeil*, no. 2, 15 Feb. 1955, pp. 5–11.

Pach, Walter. *Masters of Modern Art*. New York, 1924.

Revol, Jean. "Braque et Villon, message vivant du Cubisme." *N.R.F.*, August and September, 1961 (reprint).

Stahly, François. "Jacques Villon, His Graphic Work." *Graphis*, vol. 10, no. 53, 1954, pp. 230–237.

Vallier, Dora. *Jacques Villon, oeuvres de 1897 à 1956*. Paris (n.d.)

Villon, Jacques. "Jacques Villon: printmaker." *Art News*, October 1953, pp. 39 ff.

————"Un travail solitaire dans un chemin privé." *Arts*, no. 819, 26 Apr.-2 May, 1961.

Vieillard, Roger. "Les gravures de Jacques Villon." *Jardin des Arts*, May 1959, no. 5, pp. 446–450.

Exhibition Catalogues

Institute of Contemporary Art. *Jacques Villon–Lyonel Feininger*. Boston, 1949.

Musée National d'Art Moderne. *Jacques Villon*. Paris, 1951.

Galerie Louis Carré. *Jacques Villon, oeuvre gravé*. Paris, 1954.

Musée Toulouse-Lautrec. *Jacques Villon, peintures*. Albi, 1955.

Galerie Louis Carré. *Dessins de Jacques Villon*. Paris, 1956.

Solomon R. Guggenheim Museum. *Jacques Villon, Raymond Duchamp-Villon, Marcel Duchamp*. New York, 1957.

Institut Français d'Athènes. *Jacques Villon, gravures, dessins, aquarelles*. Athens, 1958.

Bibliothèque Nationale. *Jacques Villon, l'oeuvre gravé*. Paris, 1959.

Kunstnernes Hus. *Jacques Villon*. Oslo, 1959.

Moderna Museet. *Jacques Villon, Måleri och Grafik 1902–1959*. Stockholm, 1960.

Galerie Charpentier. *Cent tableaux de Jacques Villon*. Paris, 1961 (2 editions, regular and deluxe).

Kunsthaus. *Jacques Villon*. Zurich, 1963.

Galerie Louis Carré. *La figure dans l'oeuvre graphique de Jacques Villon*. Paris, 1963.

R. M. Light & Co.–Helene C. Seiferheld Inc. *Jacques Villon, Master Printmaker*. New York, Feb. 1964.

catalogue

The abbreviation A.&P. refers to Auberty and Pérussaux, *Jacques Villon, catalogue de son oeuvre gravé*, (Paul Prouté, 1950).

*1. PORTRAIT DE SON PERE. 1891
Etching touched with black crayon, pen and ink. 5 3/8 x 4 3/4 in. (A.&P. 1)
In pencil *portrait de mon père – mon premier gravure 1891*.
One of two impressions of Villon's first etching.
Anonymous Loan

*2. PORTRAIT DU PEINTRE-GRAVURE, EMILE NICOLLE, grand-père de l'artiste. 1891
Etching. 6 15/16 x 5 in. Epreuve d'artiste. (A.&P. 2)
Boston Public Library

Villon said of his grandfather: "Mon grand-père avait pour moi une influence de témoin, mais il ne me donnait pas de conseils."

3. DANSEUSE ESPAGNOLE. 1899
Aquatint, in dark brown. 19 7/8 x 14 in. (A.&P. 5)
Lent by Museum of Modern Art, New York. Purchase Fund.

The dancer's mother, seated in the background, watches her daughter complacently.

4. DANSEUSE ESPAGNOLE. 1899
Color aquatint in green, red, brown and black. Bon à tiré. Dedicated to Delâtre. (A.&P. 5)
Lent by Sidney Elliott Cohn

For preparatory study for this and the previous print see cat. 141.

5. BERNADETTE. 1899
Color aquatint in black, green, brown and purple. 14 5/8 x 11 in. 7/30. (A.&P. 6)
Museum of Fine Arts, Boston. Lee M. Friedman Fund. 63.1013

For several years a favorite model of Villon.

6. LA FEMME AU MANNEQUIN. 1899
Color aquatint in tan, black and gray with touches of water color in red and blue. 11 5/16 x 17 5/8 in. (A.&P. 7)
Lent by Museum of Modern Art, New York. Gift of Jean Dieniau

7. LE VIOLINISTE SUPERVIELLE. 1899
Aquatint in red. 23 3/4 x 13 5/16 in. (A.&P. 8)
Boston Public Library

The violinist was a friend of the artist.

8. DANSEUSE AU MOULIN ROUGE. 1899
Color lithograph. 11 5/8 x 9 5/8 in. Trial proof in red, yellow, blue black. Printed as a supplement to the review *L'Estampe et l'Affiche*. (A.&P. 396)
Boston Public Library

*9. GUINGUETTE FLEURIE. 1899
faubourg Montmartre, manège central, 4 Rue Buffault, chaque soir à 8. h 1/2, la fleur des poètes chansonniers montmartrois.
Poster. Color lithograph in red, yellow and dark olive. 49 3/8 x 36 3/8 in. (A.&P. 458)
Imp. d'Art Malfeyt & Cie., 8 rue Fontaine
Lent by Robert B. Appleton

*10. L'ANTI-BELIER. 1899
A. Cruchon, 29 Rue Grenier, St. Lazare
Poster. Color lithograph in red, dark green and black.
Signed on the stone: *Jacques Villon /99*. 23 3/8 x 16 3/4 in. (Not in A.&P.)
Imp. d'Art Malfeyt & Cie., 8 rue Fontaine
Lent by Richard Cox Cowell
Probably for an advertisement of perfume or eau-de-cologne.

11. MAJOR ANGLAIS. 1900
Color aquatint in yellow, green, salmon-pink and black. 9 x 4 3/4 in. 8/30. (A.&P. 12)
Boston Public Library

12. OHE! LA CLASSE, or LES TROIS SOLDATS. 1900
Color aquatint in red, blue and tan. 13 11/16 x 13 3/4 in. (A.&P. 13)
Boston Public Library
This print is a reminiscence of Villon's military service of 1897.

13. LE MAQUILLAGE, (The Make-Up). 1900
Color aquatint in rose, yellow, blue, olive-green, red-brown and black. 13 1/4 x 10 1/8 in. (A.&P. 14)
Lent by Museum of Modern Art, New York. Purchase Fund

141. STUDY FOR DANSEUSE ESPAGNOLE. 1899. Water color

17. LE PERE NORET TUANT UN COQ. 1902·
    Etching and aquatint. 8 x 6 1/8 in. (A.&P. 36)
    Boston Public Library

    Printed for *Mon vieux lycée,* a Rouen review. Père Noret was
    the gardener and coachman of Villon's parents and was
    described by the artist as "un parent de Mme. Bovary."

*18. LA PARISIENNE. 1902
    Etching and aquatint in black. 18 13/16 x 14 11/16 in.
    (A.&P. 38)
    Undescribed early state before reduction of plate, before
    color and before elimination of all details of interior of room.
    Lower right in pencil: *à Delâtre/Jacques Villon*
    *Lent by Cleveland Museum of Art. Gift of the Print Club of
    Cleveland*

14. BOUDEUSE (Sulking). 1900
    Color aquatint in blue, gray-brown, yellow and violet.
    7 x 11 3/16 in. (A.&P. 18)
    *Museum of Fine Arts, Boston. Gift of Mr. and Mrs. Peter A.
    Wick. 58.1375*

    Same model as Bernadette (A.&P. 6), cat. 5

15. PETITE FILLE A L'ESCALIER ROUGE, 1900
    Color aquatint and drypoint in shades of salmon-pink, yellow,
    blue-green, light brown. 19 1/2 x 15 3/4 in. 6/30. (A.&P. 25)
    Lent by Museum of Modern Art, New York. Purchase Fund

*16. PREMIERS BEAUX JOURS. 1902   (Color Plate I)
    Color aquatint in shades of blue, green, red and brown.
    18 7/16 x 13 1/8 in. 3/25. (A.&P. 34)
    *Museum of Fine Arts, Boston. Bequest of W. G. Russell Allen.
    60.1280*

140. QUINQUINA OPERA. 1899. Water color

10. L'ANTI-BELIER. 1899. Poster, color lithograph

*19. LA PARISIENNE. 1902
      Color aquatint in olive green and rose. 18 1/4 x 13 1/4 in.
      (A.&P. 38)
      *Museum of Fine Arts, Boston. Lee M. Friedman Fund.
      63.438*

*20. LES CARTES. 1903   (Color Plate II)
      Color aquatint in red, pink, black, yellow and green.
      13 11/16 x 17 5/8 in. (A.&P. 44)
      Trial proof with dedication to Delâtre.
      *Museum of Fine Arts, Boston. Bequest of W. G. Russell Allen
      60.1281*

21. BOHEME AUX CHAMPS (Bibi-la-Purée). 1904
      Aquatint. 11 1/8 x 8 5/8 in. First state. 5/6. (A.&P. 50[I])
      Boston Public Library

      Bibi-la-Purée's real name was André Joseph Salis de Saglia.

He was a colorful inhabitant of Montmartre, a bootblack
who cherished a cult for Verlaine whose shirt he boasted of
always wearing.

*22. MANEGE RUE CAULAINCOURT. 1904   (Color Plate III)
      Aquatint in olive green. 15 3/8 x 19 1/2 in. (A.&P. 54)
      Boston Public Library

      This merry-go-round was installed for a time next to Villon's
      house on rue Caulaincourt.

23. NEVERS A PARIS (A provincial in Montmartre). 1904
      Drypoint and aquatint. 13 3/4 x 18 in. First state. (A.&P. 55[I])
      Boston Public Library

24. NEVERS A PARIS. 1904
      Color aquatint and drypoint in tones of blue, green, red and
      brown; touched with yellow, pink and sepia chalks.
      13 3/4 x 18 in. Proof of second state. (A.&P. 55[II])
      Boston Public Library

18. LA PARISIENNE. 1902. Etching and aquatint. Undescribed early state

19. LA PARISIENNE. 1902. Color aquatint

25. LE CAKE-WALK DES PETITES FILLES. 1904. Color aquatint

*28.   AUTRE TEMPS 1830. 1904
       Color aquatint in green, ochre, violet, blue-green, grays and
       pinks; touched. 17 1/2 x 13 3/4 in. (A.&P. 72)
       With dedication to Delâtre.
       *Museum of Fine Arts, Boston. Bequest of W. G. Russell Allen.
       60.1282*

       Pertaining to the Bal Henri Monnier as do three lithographs,
       a fan and two post cards, (A.&P. 403–405), made for the
       occasion which honored the centenary of the birth of
       Monnier (1805–1877), a contemporary of Daumier.

*29.   LE POTIN (The Gossip). 1905
       Aquatint and drypoint in olive green. 16 1/4 x 22 1/2 in.
       (A.&P. 85)
       *Museum of Fine Arts, Boston. Lee M. Friedman Fund.
       63.129*

*25.   LE CAKE-WALK DES PETITES FILLES. 1904
       Color aquatint in green, blue, pink, orange, brown and black.
       12 x 16 1/2 in. Trial proof of second state. (A.&P. 56^{II})
       *Museum of Fine Arts, Boston. Stephen Bullard Memorial
       Fund, 64.10*

 26.   LA FAUTE. 1904
       Aquatint. 15 7/16 x 12 in. (A.&P. 64)
       Boston Public Library

 27.   LA PARTIE D'ECHECS. 1904
       Drypoint and aquatint. 11 7/8 x 15 3/8 in. (A.&P. 65)
       Boston Public Library

       Villon's brother, Marcel Duchamp, the painter, and his sister,
       Suzanne, at game of chess.

28. AUTRE TEMPS–1830. 1904. Color aquatint

36. LE CONCERT SUR LE PLAGE. 1907. Etching and aquatint

30. LE REMOULEUR (The Knife Grinder). 1905
Color aquatint and etching in brown, blue, green, and purple.
9 3/4 x 6 5/8 in. 15/50. (A.&P. 87)
Boston Public Library

31. LE CYCLISTE. 1905
Color aquatint and etching in red, yellow, gray and black.
9 5/8 x 6 9/16 in. 7/50. (A.&P. 88)
Boston Public Library

32. ENFANT AU TUB. 1907
Drypoint. 9 x 7 1/2 in. Trial proof. (A.&P. 108)
Museum of Modern Art, New York. Purchase Fund

33. LA MER VIENT A NOUS, TANDIS QUE LA MONTAGNE . . .
1907
Etching and aquatint. 9 3/8 x 6 7/8 in. (A.&P. 114)
Boston Public Library

34. MINNE REFLECHISSANT. 1907
Etching and softground. 9 11/16 x 6 9/16 in. 7/30.
(A.&P. 123)
Museum of Fine Arts, Boston. Gift of Mr. and Mrs. Samuel Glaser. 59.262

One of a series of 13 prints "Le Bain de Minne." The model

was the daughter of a cousin of Villon who also posed for
Renée à Bicyclette and *Renée au Canapé* (A.&P. 107, 111)
as well as the later series (A.&P. 180–183). See cats. 45–47.

35. LES FEMMES DE THRACE. 1907
Etching. 8 1/2 x 6 1/2 in. 8/30. (A.&P. 119)
Boston Public Library

See drawing, cat. 144.

*36. LE CONCERT SUR LE PLAGE. 1907
Etching and aquatint. 8 5/8 x 7 3/4 in. 48/50. (A.&P. 138)
Boston Public Library

*37. JEUNE FEMME AU PIANO. 1908
Drypoint. 20 x 15 1/2 in. 15/25. (A.&P. 144)
Boston Public Library

*38. YVONNE AUX MAINS CROISEES. 1908
Drypoint. 15 1/2 x 11 7/8 in. 18/25. (A.&P. 151)
Boston Public Library

Sister of the artist.

39. ENFANT AU PIANO. 1909
Drypoint. 15 3/4 x 11 7/8 in. 15/16. (A.&P. 158)
Boston Public Library

29. LE POTIN (The Gossip). 1905. Aquatint and drypoint

Boston Public Library
The model who posed for cat. 34 (A.&P. 123) and for cats. 46, 47 (A.&P. 181 and 183).

*46.   RENEE DE TROIS QUARTS. 1911
Drypoint. 22 1/16 x 16 1/8 in. 24/30. (A.&P. 181)
Lent by Galerie Louis Carré

A painting, illus. Vallier p. 37, is dated 1908–9.

47.   PETITE MULATRESSE. 1911
Etching. 9 x 7 3/8 in. 27/50. (A.&P. 183)
Boston Public Library

*48.   MUSICIENS CHEZ LE BISTRO. 1912
Etching. 10 1/2 x 9 1/8 in. 14/50. (A.&P. 185)
Boston Public Library

40.   SUR LE COCHONS. 1909
Drypoint and softground etching. 15 1/2 x 12 in. First state.
(A.&P. 159^I)
Boston Public Library

*41.   NU DEBOUT, BRAS EN L'AIR. 1909
Drypoint. 21 5/8 x 16 11/16 in. 5/23. (A.&P. 163)
Museum of Fine Arts, Boston. Lee M. Friedman Fund. 61.613

42.   NU COUCHE. 1909
Drypoint and aquatint. 13 5/8 x 18 in. 12/20. (A.&P. 164)
Boston Public Library

43.   GIRL WITH CATS. 1909
Etching, drypoint and softground. 9 3/8 x 6 5/8 in. 22/30.
(Not in A.&P.)
Lent by Yale University Art Gallery, Collection of the Société Anonyme

44.   FEMME ASSISE NUE. 1910
Drypoint. 15 3/8 x 12 in. 11/15. (A.&P. 165)
Lent by Museum of Modern Art, New York. Larry Aldrich Fund

45.   RENEE DE FACE. 1911
Drypoint (large plate). 18 x 13 9/16 in. Epreuve d'artiste.
(A.&P. 180)

37. JEUNE FEMME AU PIANO. 1908. Drypoint

38. YVONNE AUX MAINS CROISEES. 1908. Drypoint

46. RENEE DE TROIS QUARTS. 1911. Drypoint

49. PORTRAIT DE FELIX BARRE. 1913
Drypoint. 6 5/8 x 5 3/8 in. (A.&P. 189)
Boston Public Library

See cat. 56 (A.&P. 199)

*50. PORTRAIT DE E. D. (Artist's father). 1913
Etching and drypoint. 9 1/4 x 6 1/4 in. 11/25. (A.&P. 191)
Museum of Fine Arts, Boston. Gift of Peter A. Wick. 53.2216

In the Guggenheim Museum there is a painting of Villon's
father dated 1924, a late reflection of cubism but not in
profile, illus. Guggenheim cat. 1957.

51. PORTRAIT DE JEUNE FEMME. 1913
Drypoint. 21 1/2 x 16 3/16 in. 12/50. (A.&P. 193)
Lower right in pencil: à *Madame Roosevelt / cordialement /
Jacques Villon*
Museum of Fine Arts, Boston. Samuel P. Avery Fund. 55.933

*52. YVONNE D. DE PROFIL. 1913
Drypoint. 21 5/8 x 16 5/16 in. First state. 3/11.
(A.&P. 194^I)
Boston Public Library

53. JEUNE FILLE DE PROFIL. 1913
Wood engraving. 6 1/4 x 4 9/16 in. (A.&P. 454)
Boston Public Library

*54. LA TABLE SERVIE. 1913
Drypoint. 11 3/16 x 15 3/16 in. First state. 1/30. (A.&P.
196^I)
Lent by R. G. Michel

A painting illus. Vallier p. 43 and dated 1913 is in the coll. of
Mr. and Mrs. F. Steegmuller; another painting is in the Yale
University Art Gallery, Collection Société Anonyme, dated
1912/13. A series of four drawings dated 1912 also illus.
Vallier, pp. 44 and 45. The print was exhibited at the Salon
d'Automne, 1913.

48. MUSICIENS CHEZ LE BISTRO. 1912. Etching

50. PORTRAIT DE E. D. (Artist's Father). 1913. Etching

52. YVONNE D. DE PROFIL. 1913. Drypoint

58. LE PETIT ATELIER DE MECANIQUE. 1914
Etching. 6 1/8 x 7 9/16 in. (A.&P. 202)
Boston Public Library

See related paintings: fragment, 1914, coll. Edwin Stein,
N.Y. (illus. Vallier p. 49); same title, 1914 Columbus Gallery
of Fine Arts; another, 1946, Phillips Collection (illus. Galerie
Charpentier 1961); *Atelier de Mecanique, Tintamare,* 1947,
coll. Léon Duesberg, Verviers (illus. Vallier p. 82); *Un Atelier
de Mécanique,* 1955, coll. Louis Carré (illus. Vallier p. 103).

*59. TABLE D'ECHECS. 1920
Etching. 8 x 6 1/4 in. (A.&P. 203)
*Lent by Museum of Modern Art, New York. Gift of Ludwig
Charell*

First plate made by Villon after World War I. It was destined
for a German review in which Gleizes and others collaborated.
Recently a Parisian print dealer discovered a number of
proofs in Germany.
See drawing, 1919, cat. 151; painting, 1919, coll. Louis
Carré (illus. Vallier, p. 51).

*60. BAUDELAIRE AVEC SOCLE. 1920
After a bust by Duchamp-Villon of 1911.
Etching. 16 5/16 x 11 1/16 in. 20/50. (A.&P. 204)
*Museum of Fine Arts, Boston. Bequest of W. G. Russell Allen.
60.1284*

The sculpture was exhibited at the Armory Show, 1913.
See drawing, cat. 154, and terra cotta, cat. 191.

*55. M. D. (UCHAMP) LISANT. 1913
Drypoint. 15 3/8 x 11 9/16 in. 1/32. (A.&P. 198)
Lent by Mr. and Mrs. Samuel Glaser

*56. PORTRAIT D'ACTEUR (Felix Barré). 1913
Drypoint. 15 3/4 x 12 3/8 in. 31/32. (A.&P. 199)
Boston Public Library

See cat. 49 (A.&P. 189) and drawing, 1919, cat. 152.
Villon also made an engraving of this subject (A.&P. 190)
the drawing for which is illus. pl. 19, *20th Century Master
Drawings,* Guggenheim-University of Minnesota-Fogg
museums, 1963–1964, cat. 119. See also three paintings,
1912 and 1913, illus. Vallier pp. 40, 41.

*57. LE PETIT EQUILIBRISTE. 1914
Etching. 8 5/8 x 6 7/16 in. (A.&P. 201)
Boston Public Library

Published in Lassaigne, *Eloge de Jacques Villon,* Paris,
Bruker, 1955. See drawing, cat. 147.
The subject absorbed Villon constantly. He made a drypoint,
Equilibriste, 1913 (A.&P. 197); two paintings, both dated
1913, illus. Vallier pp. 46 and 48; and a later painting,
Equilibre Rouge, 1921, illus. Vallier opp. p. 16.

55. M. D. (uchamp) LISANT. 1913. Drypoint

152. POUR UN PORTRAIT DE BARRE. 1919. Pencil and water color

56. PORTRAIT D'ACTEUR (Félix Barré). 1913. Drypoint

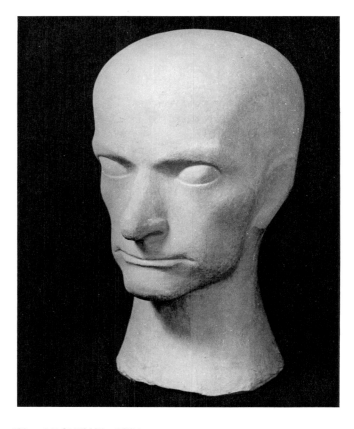

*61. LE CHEVAL. 1921
      Etching. 3 1/8 x 5 1/8 in. Epreuve d'artiste. (A.&P. 206)
      Lent by Galerie Louis Carré
      Published in Gleizes and Metzinger, *Du Cubisme,* 1947.
      See drawings, cats. 157–167.

*62. SUR LES ROCHERS. 1927
      Etching. 8 3/4 x 10 3/4 in. Second state. 5/50. (A.&P.
      212^{II})
      Boston Public Library

*63. DAGUERREOTYPE NO. 1. 1927
      Etching. 6 1/4 x 8 5/8 in. 22/50. (A.&P. 214)
      *Museum of Fine Arts, Boston. Gift of Mr. and Mrs. Peter A.
      Wick. 56.1133*

64.   DAGUERREOTYPE NO. 2. 1927
      Etching. 6 11/16 x 8 3/4 in. 22/50. (A.&P. 215)
      *Museum of Fine Arts, Boston. Gift of Mr. and Mrs. Peter A.
      Wick. 56.1134*

65.   L'ITALIENNE. 1927
      After painting by Modigliani of 1916.
      Color aquatint. 19 9/16 x 12 1/8 in. (A.&P. 517)
      Published by Chalcographie du Louvre
      Museum of Fine Arts, Boston. Lee M. Friedman Fund. 58.137
      This represents the kind of work Villon was obliged to do
      when under financial strain.

66.   COMPOSITION. 1928
      Color aquatint and roulette in yellow, red, orange-brown and
      black. 19 1/4 x 13 3/8 in. 126/200. (A.&P. 526)
      Lent by Fogg Art Museum, Harvard University

      See painting, *Composition-figure,* 1920, coll. Louis Suë, illus.
      Lassaigne, *Jacques Villon,* 1950, Pl. VIII.

*67. TETE DE FILLETTE. 1929
      Drypoint. 10 3/4 x 8 5/16 in. First state. 44/50. (A.&P. 217^{I})
      Boston Public Library

*68. TETE DE FILLETTE. 1929
      Etching. 10 3/4 x 8 5/16 in. Second state. 37/50. (A.&P.
      217^{II})
      Boston Public Library

191. by Raymond Duchamp-Villon. PORTRAIT DE BAUDELAIRE. 1911. Terra cotta

60. BAUDELAIRE AVEC SOCLE. 1920. Etching

61. LE CHEVAL. 1921. Etching

62. SUR LES ROCHERS. 1927. Etching

69. L'ECOLIERE LISANT (The Student Reading). 1929
    Etching. 10 3/4 x 8 3/4 in. 33/50. (A.&P. 218)
    *Lent by Museum of Modern Art, New York. Lillie P. Bliss
    Bequest*

*70. HOMME LISANT. 1929
    Etching. 10 3/8 x 8 11/16 in. Epreuve d'artiste (A.&P. 219)
    Lent by Galerie Louis Carré

*71. NATURE MORTE AU NOIX. 1929
    Etching. 8 3/4 x 10 7/8 in. Second state. 37/50 (A.&P.
    220[II])
    Museum of Fine Arts, Boston. Gift of Peter A. Wick. 53.2214

    A painting, 1927, private coll., exhibited 1951, Musée
    National d'Art Moderne, cat. 24.

72. LES HALEURS. 1930
    Drypoint. 7 1/16 x 8 3/4 in. First state. (A.&P. 222[I])
    Boston Public Library

    Villon was struck one day by the effort of a group of workmen
    hauling a cable on the banks of the Seine. In 1907 he made an
    aquatint of this subject (A.&P. 120) and in 1908 an oil paint-
    ing illus. Galerie Charpentier 1961 in private coll. The two
    prints of 1930 are examples of the way in which Villon often
    returned to a subject radically transforming it in style.

*73. LES HALEURS. 1930
    Etching and drypoint. 7 1/16 x 8 3/4 in. Second state.
    25/30. (A.&P. 222[II])
    Boston Public Library

74. LA MARIEE. 1930
    Color aquatint after the painting by Marcel Duchamp, 1912.
    19 1/2 x 12 5/16 in. 148/200. (Not in A.&P.)
    Lent by R.M. Light and Co., Inc.

    The painting is in the Arensberg Collection, Philadelphia
    Museum of Art.

75. LES VINGT ANS FIERS. 1930–31
    Etching and drypoint. 5 15/16 x 8 1/2 in. Second state.
    (A.&P. 227[II])
    Boston Public Library
    See drawing, cat. 172.

    The title comes from a poem by Veillé-Griffin, "La Partenza."

76. HEAD OF A MAN (Self-Portrait). 1930
    Etching. 7 1/4 x 6 in. 4/50. (A.&P. 228)
    *Museum of Fine Arts, Boston. Gift of Mr. and Mrs. Peter A.
    Wick. 56.1135*

63. DAGUERREOTYPE, NO. I. 1927. Etching

*77. NATURE MORTE AU PERROQUET. 1932
Etching and drypoint. 8 3/4 x 11 1/8 in. First state. 4/15.
(A.&P. 247^I)
Museum of Fine Arts, Boston. Gift of Peter A. Wick. 53.2217

See drawing, cat. 173.

78. NATURE MORTE AU PERROQUET. 1934
Etching and roulette and burin. 8 3/4 x 11 1/8 in. Second
state. Epreuve d'artiste. (A.&P. 247^{II})
Boston Public Library

Related to painting, *Nature Morte à la Poussière*, 1933.

79. LE JUIF ERRANT. 1932
Drypoint. 9 x 6 1/2 in. Epreuve d'artiste. (A.&P. 250)
Boston Public Library

80. LE SAVANT (J. P. Dubray). 1933
Etching. 11 3/8 x 9 1/8 in. Epreuve d'artiste. (A.&P. 254)
Boston Public Library

See drawings cats. 174, 175.
Jean Paul Dubray (1888–1940) painter-engraver and
author.

*81. NOTRE DAME DE VIE. 1934
Etching. 7 x 10 1/4 in. Second state. 22/30. (A.&P. 263^{II})

Boston Public Library
See drawing, cat. 176.
See painting dated 1944 of same subject in coll. Mme.
Robert Philippe, illus. Charpentier cat. 1961.

*82. LE GRAND DESSINATEUR ASSIS (Self-Portrait). 1935
Etching and drypoint. 10 7/16 x 7 7/8 in. Essai. (A.&P. 266)
Lent by Galerie Louis Carré

See drawing, cat. 178.

*83. LE PETIT DESSINATEUR. (Self-Portrait). 1935
Etching. 6 3/8 x 4 3/4 in. 9/50. (A.&P. 267)
Boston Public Library

See painting cat. 190 and drawing cat. 179.

*84. CHEVREUSE (TOUR DE FRANCE). 1935
Etching. 8 1/4 x 10 1/2 in. First state with cyclists. 15/25.
(A.&P. 272^I)
Museum of Fine Arts, Boston. Gift of Peter A. Wick. 53.2215

In the second state Villon removed the cyclists and added
some intersecting lines which make the composition more
abstract.
In 1953 Villon said to Russel Warren Howe "I prefer landscape to still life. Landscape has . . . movement . . . landscape
suggests eternity."

173. NATURE MORTE AU PERROQUET. 1932. Pen, red and India ink and pencil

77. NATURE MORTE AU PERROQUET. 1932. Etching and drypoint

179. STUDY FOR LE PETIT DESSINATEUR (Self-Portrait). 1935. Pen and India ink

83. LE PETIT DESSINATEUR (Self-Portrait). 1935. Etching

84. CHEVREUSE (Tour de France). 1935. Etching

88. L'USINE. 1935. Etching

86. F. STEEGMULLER. 1935. Etching

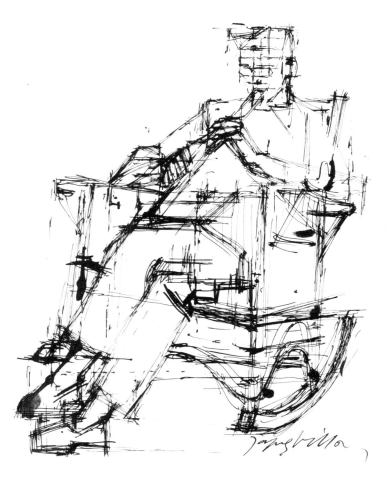

*95. LES TROIS ORDRES: LE CHATEAU, L'EGLISE,
      LA CAMPAGNE. 1939
      Etching. 11 3/16 x 7 3/8 in. 41/50. (A.&P. 325)
      Boston Public Library

      See painting dated 1944, coll. Louis Carré, illus. Vallier p. 77.

96.   D'OU ON TOURNE L'EPAULE A LA VIE. 1939
      Etching. 8 3/8 x 10 1/4 in. 35/40. (A.&P. 327)
      Boston Public Library

      This print is an allegory inspired by "Fenêtres" of Mallarmé.
      It is in reverse of a painting of same title, dated 1938, coll.
      Mme. Robert Blay, illus. Vallier, p. 70.

*91. LE JOUEUR DE FLAGEOLET. 1938
      Etching and drypoint. 8 1/8 x 6 1/4 in. Epreuve d'artiste.
      (A.&P. 314)
      Boston Public Library

      See drawing cat. 181.

*92. L'APPEL DE LA VIE (les filles). 1938
      Etching. 14 7/8 x 11 1/8 in. 14/40. (A.&P. 320)
      Boston Public Library

*93. LA BAIE DU PETIT SALON. 1938
      Etching. 10 5/8 x 8 9/16 in. 23/50. (A.&P. 321)
      Boston Public Library

      See painting of same title, dated 1943, more abstract in
      style, coll. Louis Carré, illus. Oslo cat., 1959.

94.   LE PONT DE BEAUGENCY. 1939
      Etching and drypoint. 12 7/16 x 8 1/2 in. 36/45. (A.&P. 323)
      Boston Public Library

      See painting dated 1940–41, Louis Carré coll. illus. Vallier
      p. 76.

181. LE JOUEUR DE FLAGEOLET. ca. 1938–39 (?) Pen and India ink

91. LE JOUEUR DE FLAGEOLET. 1938. Etching and drypoint

171. SEATED BOY. 1922. Pen and India ink

92. L'APPEL DE LA VIE (Les Filles). 1938. Etching

100. JEUNE FILLE. 1942. Engraving

101. INTERIEUR. 1943. Etching

102. UNE GRAND-MERE. 1943. Drypoint

97. L'EFFORT. 1939
Etching. 11 5/8 x 9 3/8 in. 44/50. (A.&P. 328)
Boston Public Library

A painting, same date, private coll. listed in Lassaigne, 1950.

*98. LA LUTTE. 1939
Etching and drypoint. 11 1/16 x 9 13/16 in. Epreuve
d'artiste. 6/10. (A.&P. 329)
Lent by Galerie Louis Carré

A painting, *Les Lutteurs*, 1939, coll. Louis Carré in Oslo cat.
1959, no. 29, and another, *La Lutte, le Chaos*, 1939, coll.
Herr Haakon Onstad, in same, no. 31.

*99. CALIBAN. 1941
Engraving and drypoint. 8 1/16 x 6 3/4 in. Proof. (A.&P. 333)
Lent by Galerie Louis Carré

A painting of 1936, Musée National d'Art Moderne, cat.
no. 41, coll. M. René Bauret.

*100. JEUNE FILLE. 1942
Engraving. 11 1/8 x 8 1/16 in. Epreuve d'artiste. (A.&P.
335)
Boston Public Library

*101. INTERIEUR. 1943
Etching. 10 1/2 x 8 5/8 in. 14/40. (A.&P. 340)
Boston Public Library

*102. UNE GRAND-MERE (the mother of Mme. Mare). 1943
Drypoint. 9 11/16 x 7 in. 25/45. (A.&P. 341)
Boston Public Library

There exists a painting of 1939, (see Bibliotèque Nationale,
cat. 122).

*103. GLOBE CELESTE, LE CIEL. 1944
Etching. 11 1/8 x 8 1/8 in. Epreuve d'artiste. (A.&P. 347)
Lent by Peter Deitsch Gallery

*104. CAMILLE RENAULT. 1945
Etching. 15 7/8 x 12 3/8 in. Third state. (A.&P. 358[III])
*Museum of Fine Arts, Boston. Lee M. Friedman Fund.
63.1301*

Owner of a restaurant at Puteaux and a loyal friend of
Villon.
There exists a painting (see Bibliotèque Nationale, cat.
132).

104. CAMILLE RENAULT. 1945. Etching

105. PORTRAIT DE MLLE. GOERG. 1947. Etching

103. GLOBE CELESTE, LE CIEL. 1944. Etching

*105. PORTRAIT DE MLLE. GOERG. 1947
Etching. 8 5/8 x 6 1/4 in. Epreuve d'artiste. (A.&P. 361)
Boston Public Library

Daughter of the peintre-graveur, Edouard Goerg.

106. LES ARPETES (The Apprentices). 1947
Etching. 9 3/8 x 7 3/8 in. Second state, plate cut. 12/25.
(A.&P. 362[II])
Boston Public Library

*107. LE SACRE-COEUR 1900. 1948
Etching. 7 13/16 x 10 15/16 in. 14/45. (A.&P. 375)
Boston Public Library

After a drawing made in 1899 at which time Sacré-Coeur
was not yet completed and was surrounded by scaffolding.
The composition was used in 1900 by Villon for the back-
drop of a cabaret into which he substituted the existing
pipes for the wooden scaffolding.

*108. LA CATHEDRALE (de Rouen). 1948
Etching and drypoint. 11 3/4 x 7 3/4 in. 8/50. (A.&P. 376)
Boston Public Library

*109. LES DEUX VASES. 1950
Engraving. 8 1/4 x 6 1/8 in. 30/40. (Not in A.&P.)

Pub. Lassaigne, *Eloge de Jacques Villon,* Bruker, 1955
Lent by Galerie Louis Carré

A painting titled *Vers la Chimère,* dated 1947 is similar,
private coll., illus. Charpentier cat. 1961, no. 68.

*110. LES LAMPES. 1951
Etching and color aquatint printed in blue, green, yellow,
orange, rose, lavender and black. 9 9/16 x 10 3/4 in. 39/40.
(Not in A.&P.)
Lent by Galerie Louis Carré

*111. GEOMETRIE. 1951
Etching. 9 1/16 x 7 7/8 in. 17/30. (Not in A.&P.)
Lent by Galerie Louis Carré

*112. LA SIGNATURE – PORTRAIT OF THE ARTIST. 1951
Etching and drypoint. 8 1/8 x 6 9/16 in. 2/25. (Not in A.&P.)
*Lent by Museum of Modern Art, New York. Gift of Hubert de
Givenchy*

Sometimes called *The Usurer.*
Painting of 1949, coll. Louis Carré, illus. Charpentier cat.
1961 and another, same date, Carnegie Institute, Pittsburgh,
illus. Guggeheim cat. of 1957. A drawing illus. *Emporium,*
Vol. CXXIII, 1956, p. 229.

108. LA CATHEDRALE (de Rouen). 1948. Etching and drypoint

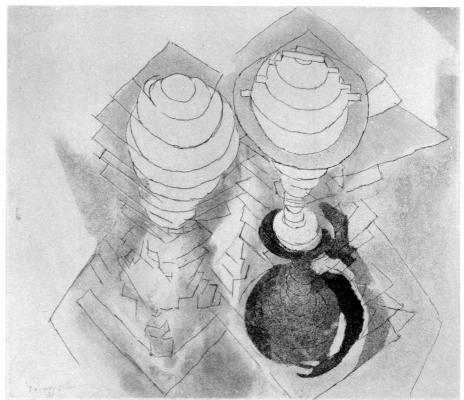

109. LES DEUX VASES. 1950. Engraving

111. GEOMETRIE. 1951. Etching

110. LES LAMPES. 1951. Etching and color aquatint

113. LA COLERE. 1952
Etching. 12 3/8 x 9 1/8 in. 43/60. (Not in A.&P.)
Lent by Ferdinand Roten Gallery

See drawing cat. 185.

*114. L'UNIVERS. 1951   (Color Plate IV)
Color aquatint printed in yellow, orange-brown, red, green,
blue and black. 7 3/16 x 6 7/8 in. (Not in A.&P.)
Lent by Mr. and Mrs. Samuel Glaser

115. PORTRAIT DE MARCEL DUCHAMP. 1953
Etching. 12 3/8 x 9 11/16 in. 1/10. Epreuve d'artiste.
(Not in A.&P.)
*Lent by Museum of Modern Art, New York. Gift of Louis
Carré*

See drawing cat. 186.

*116. MATERNITE.
Etching. 11 x 7 3/8 in. 65/75. (Not in A.&P.)
Boston Public Library

Painting of 1948 illus. Vallier, coll. Ira Haupt; another of
same date illus. Oslo cat. 1959 coll. Sonja Henie, with title
La Grande Maternité.

117. L'ATRE (or Le Fauteuil)
Color lithograph in red, blue, green, yellow, gray and black.
19 x 11 7/8 in. Epreuve d'artiste. (Not in A.&P.)
*Museum of Fine Arts, Boston. Bequest of W. G. Russell
Allen. 60.1286*

See painting of 1954. Coll. Léon Duesberg, illus. Vallier,
p. 100 and painting of 1955, Galerie Louis Carré, illus.
Vallier, p. 107.

118. L'ECUYERE.
Color lithograph in shades of yellow, green, blue, rose.
12 x 17 1/2 in. 109/200. (Not in A.&P.)
Lent by Fogg Art Museum, Harvard University

A painting of same title, dated 1951, coll. Louis Carré, exh.
Musée National d'Art Moderne, 1951, no. 84.

119-123. LES YEUX FUTILES. ca. 1956
Series of five proofs, including a trial proof of the final
state for a print used in P. Eluard, *Un Poème dans Chaque*

Livre, Paris, Editions L. Broder, 1956. The print also
appeared as Pl. 16 in *Estampes Originales, Album A,*
Paris, L. Broder, Editeur, 1956.

119. Les yeux futiles, No. 1
Etching. 6 x 5 3/4 in. Epreuve d'essai in black and white.
(Not in A.&P.)
*Museum of Fine Arts, Boston. Gift of Mr. and Mrs. Peter A.
Wick. 58.1376*

120. Les yeux futiles, No. 2
Etching. 6 x 5 3/4 in. Epreuve d'état. Color separation in
red and yellow. (Not in A.&P.)
*Museum of Fine Arts, Boston. Gift of Mr. and Mrs. Peter A.
Wick. 58.1377*

121. Les yeux futiles, No. 3
Etching. 6 x 5 3/4 in. Epreuve d'état, combining black and
white with yellow and red. (Not in A.&P.)
*Museum of Fine Arts, Boston. Gift of Mr. and Mrs. Peter A.
Wick. 58.1378*

122. Les yeux futiles, No. 4
Aquatint in green. 6 x 5 3/4 in. Epreuve d'état of back-
ground color separation. (Not in A.&P.)
*Museum of Fine Arts, Boston. Gift of Mr. and Mrs. Peter A.
Wick. 58.1379*

112. LA SIGNATURE (Portrait of the Artist). 1951. Etching and drypoint

*123. Les yeux futiles, No. 5   (Color Plate V)
Etching and aquatint in red, yellow, blue and black.
6 x 5 3/4 in. Epreuve d'essai for the final state. (Not in A.&P.)
Museum of Fine Arts, Boston. Gift of Mr. and Mrs. Peter A. Wick. 58.1380

124. CONQUETE DE L'AIR (Birds in Flight). 1958
Color lithograph in shades of blue, red, yellow, green and orange. 11 7/8 x 16 in. Proof. (Not in A.&P.)
Lent by Museum of Modern Art, New York. Gift of Gérald Cramer

A painting of this subject, vertical in composition, dated 1947, private coll., illus. Vallier, p. 69.

illustrated books

125. IMPRESSIONS. Jacques Villon
Paris, Edmond Sagot, 1907.
10 color lithographs and cover. (A.&P. 409–418)
Without text.
Lent by Mrs. St. John Smith

126. POESIES. Pierre Corrard
Paris, Librairie J. Meyniel, 1937
16 etchings. (A.&P. 287–303)
Lent by Harvard College Library, Division of Printing and Graphic Arts. Gift of Philip Hofer

127. LES MYSTERES DE PARIS. André Frénaud
Paris, Editions du Seuil, 1945
Drypoint frontispiece. (A.&P. 342)
Lent by Harvard College Library, Division of Printing and Graphic Arts. Gift of Philip Hofer

*128. CANTIQUE SPIRITUEL. Jean Racine
Paris, Raoul Mortier, 1945
5 etchings. (A.&P. 349–353)
Lent by Mr. and Mrs. Samuel Glaser

128. Plate from CANTIQUE SPIRITUEL, Jean Racine. 1945. Etching

Color Plate V. LES YEUX FUTILES. 1956. Color aquatint

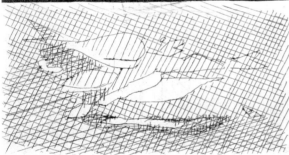

131. LAUS VENERIS. Algernon Charles Swinburne
     Paris, Editions Manuel Bruker, 1956
     10 etchings.
     Lent by The New York Public Library, Spencer Collection

*132. OEUVRE POETIQUE. Robert Ganzo
     Paris, Edition Marcel Sautier, 1957
     8 etchings.
     Lent by Mr. and Mrs. Samuel Glaser

133. A POEMES ROMPUS. Max Jacob
     Paris, Louis Broder, 1960
     5 etchings and aquatints in color; 1 etching in black.
     Lent by The New York Public Library, Spencer Collection

*134. LES TRAVAUX ET LES JOURS. Hésiode
     Paris, Tériade, 1962
     19 etchings and 4 color aquatints
     Lent by Mr. and Mrs. Samuel Glaser

129. POEMES DE BRANDEBOURG. André Frénaud
     Paris, La Nouvelle Revue Française, 1947
     6 color etchings. (A.&P. 367–372)
     Museum of Fine Arts, Boston. Gift of Mr. and Mrs. Peter A.
     Wick. 57.158

     See drawings cats. 183 and 184.

130. LES BUCOLIQUES DE VIRGILE. P. Valéry
     Paris, Scripta & Picta, 1955
     27 color lithographs
     Lent by Mr. and Mrs. Samuel Glaser

130 bis. LA SOIF DU JONC. Tiggie Ghika
     Paris, Editions des Cahiers d'Art, 1955
     3 drypoints.
     Lent by Mr. and Mrs. Joseph M. Edinburg

132. Plate from OEUVRE POETIQUE, Robert Ganzo. 1957. Etching

134. Plate from LES TRAVAUX ET LES JOURS, Hésiode. 1962. Etching

drawings and water colors

135. LA FEMME CHIC. 1894–1904
Water color and black crayon. 9 x 5 1/8 in.
Lower left in pencil: *Jacques Villon.*
Repr. in facsimile in *Jacques Villon, Cent Croquis 1894–1904,* Paris, P. Berès, 1959.
Lent by Sidney Elliott Cohn

136. UN BAR CHIC AUX CHAMPS ELYSEES. 1894–1904
Water color and black crayon. 6 3/4 x 4 3/4 in.
Lower left in pencil: *Jacques Villon.*
Repr. in facsimile in *Jacques Villon, Cent Croquis 1894–1904,* Paris, P. Berès, 1959.
Lent by Sidney Elliott Cohn

137. LUCIE. 1894–1904
Black crayon. 7 5/8 x 5 1/8 in.
Lower right in pencil: *Jacques Villon.*
Repr. in facsimile in: *Jacques Villon, Cent Croquis 1894–1904,* Paris, P. Berès, 1959.
Lent by Sidney Elliott Cohn

*138. AU RESTAURANT. ca. 1897
Water color and black crayon. 7 3/4 x 4 5/8 in.
Lower right in pencil: *J. Villon.*
Anonymous loan, courtesy of Peter Deitsch

*139. MAIS QU'EST CE-QU'ON JOUAIT DONC DIMANCHE DERNIER? (The poet). 1899
Black and blue crayons and India ink. 18 1/8 x 12 3/16 in.
Lower right in black crayon: *Jacques Villon.*
Lent by Peter Deitsch Gallery

*140. QUINQUINA OPERA. 1899
Water color over crayon. 11 13/16 x 9 7/16 in.
At right in wash: *Jacques Villon / 99.*
Lent by Peter Deitsch

Study for an unexecuted poster.

*141. STUDY FOR DANSEUSE ESPAGNOL. 1899
Water color and pencil. 19 5/8 x 13 7/8 in.
Lower left in wash: *Jacques Villon / 99.*
Lent by Benjamin Sonnenberg

Study for cats. 3 and 4. (A.&P. 5).

138. AU RESTAURANT. ca. 1897. Water color and crayon

142. PORTRAIT DE SON PERE. 1900
Black chalk with touches of red and blue chalk and wash.
7 1/2 x 4 1/2 in.
Upper right in pencil: *Jacques Villon / 00.*
Lent by Mr. and Mrs. Edward Powis Jones

*142 bis. FEMME LISANT. 1902
Water color and pen. 18 x 10 3/4 in.
Lower left in pen: *Jacques Villon / 02.*
Lent by Dr. and Mrs. Milton R. Sapirstein

143. CROQUIS AU PALAIS DE GLACE. ca. 1906
Brush and gray wash. 17 3/8 x 11 1/16 in.
Lower right in pencil: *Jacques Villon.*
On verso: colored chalk for transfer.
Boston Public Library

*144. LES FEMMES DE THRACE. 1907
Water color and pencil. 12 3/4 x 7 7/8 in.
Lower right in pencil: *Jacques Villon.*
Lent by Art Institute of Chicago, Regenstein Coll.

Preparatory study for etching, (A.&P. 119) cat. 35.

*145. PORTRAIT DE DUCHAMP–VILLON. 1911
Pencil. 10 3/16 x 6 11/16 in.
Lower right in pencil: *Duchamp Villon / par Jacques
Villon / 11.*
Lent by Galerie Louis Carré

See painting, 1911, Musée National de l'Art Moderne,
Paris, illus. Vallier p. 40.

*146. SOLDATS EN MARCHE. 1912
Photograph of drawing reworked in wash. 6 5/16 x 8 7/8 in.
Lower right: *Jacques Villon 1912*
Lent by Musée National d'Art Moderne, Paris

See painting, coll. Louis Carré, illus. Vallier p. 42.

*147. L'EQUILIBRISTE. 1912
Pen, red, blue and India inks over pencil on tracing paper.
8 13/16 x 6 3/8 in.
Lower right in pen over pencil: *Jacques Villon / 12.*
Lent by Galerie Louis Carré

See etching *Le petit equilibriste* (A.&P. 201) cat. 57.

142 bis. FEMME LISANT. 1902. Water color and pen

149. STUDY FOR LA FEMME ASSISE. 1914
Pen, red and India ink and pencil, touched with yellow and white gouache, on tracing paper. Squared. 15 1/4 x 8 3/4 in.
Lower right in pen over pencil: *Jacques Villon / 14*.
Lent by Galerie Louis Carré

See painting of 1914, coll. Louis Carré, illus. Galerie Charpentier (1961).

150. LE BAISER. 1918
Pen, India ink, gray wash and pencil. 8 x 10 in.
Lower left in ink: *Jacques Villon / 18* ; below: title.
Lent by Galerie Louis Carré

148. LE JARDIN PUBLIC. 1913
Photograph of drawing reworked in pen and blue-black ink.
8 3/16 x 6 5/16 in.
Lower right: *Jacques Villon / 13*.
Lent by Galerie Louis Carré

145. PORTRAIT DE DUCHAMP-VILLON. 1911. Pencil

153. FIGURE-PLANS. 1920. Pencil

*151. LA TABLE D'ECHECS. 1919
Pen, red and black ink, black, red and blue pencil.
14 x 7 1/4 in.
Lower left in black ink: *Jacques Villon 19*.
Lent by Galerie Louis Carré

See etching (A.&P. 203) cat. 59

*152. POUR UN PORTRAIT DE BARRE. 1919
Black, red and blue pencils and water color. Squared.
8 3/4 x 6 3/8 in.
Lower right in pen over pencil: *Jacques Villon / 19*.
Lent by Galerie Louis Carré

See cats. 49 and 56.

*153. FIGURE–PLANS. 1920
Pencil on tracing paper. 10 7/8 x 7 13/16 in.
Lower right: *Jacques Villon / 20*.
Lent by Galerie Louis Carré

154. BAUDELAIRE, NO. 25. 1920
Pencil and water color. Squared. 8 x 4 5/8 in.
Lower left in pencil: *Jacques Villon / 20* ; below: title.
Lent by Galerie Louis Carré

See etching (A.&P. 204), cat. 60.

155. DECOMPOSITION PAR PLANS D'UNE TETE VUE DE FACE.
1920
Pen, black ink, black and colored pencils. Squared.
12 1/4 x 9 1/4 in.
Upper center in pencil: title; lower right center: *Jacques
Villon / 1920*.
Lent by Galerie Louis Carré

*156. L'ATHLETE DE DUCHAMP-VILLON. 1921
After the sculpture by Duchamp-Villon, exhibited at Armory
Show, 1913.
Black, red and blue pencil on tracing paper. 10 13/16 x
8 7/16 in.
Lower center in black pencil: *Jacques Villon* ; below margin
center: title and *1921*.
*Museum of Fine Arts, Boston. George Peabody Gardner
Fund. 56.1189*

157-167. ELEVEN STUDIES OF HORSES related to paintings:
Galop, 1921, coll. Louis Carré (illus. Vallier p. 54); *Com-
position en Jaune et Bleu* or *Galop*, 1921, coll. Gerard
Bonnier, Stockholm (illus. Galerie Charpentier 1961);
Cheval de Course, 1922, coll. Louis Carré (illus. Galerie
Charpentier 1961); *Les Courses*, 1922, coll. Jerome Hill,
New York (illus. Vallier p. 55); *The Jockey*, 1924, Yale
University Art Gallery, coll. of the Société Anonyme; and
others.

*157. Study for *The Jockey*, No. 1. 1921
Pencil. 2 7/8 x 14 1/4 in.
Lower right in pencil: *Jacques Villon 21* ; lower left: *No. 1*.
*Lent by Yale University Art Gallery, Collection of the
Société Anonyme*

*158. Study for *The Jockey*, No. 2. 1921
Pencil. 5 7/8 x 14 1/8 in.
Lower right in pencil: *Jacques Villon 21* ; lower left: *No. 2*.
*Lent by Yale University Art Gallery, Collection of the
Société Anonyme*

159. Study for *The Jockey*, No. 3. 1921
Pencil. 12 3/4 x 16 3/8 in.
Left of center in pencil: *No. 3*.
*Lent by Yale University Art Gallery, Collection of the
Société Anonyme*

160. Study for *The Jockey*, No. 4. 1921
Pencil, pen, black and red ink and water color.
15 1/4 x 21 3/4 in.
Lower right in pencil: *Jacques Villon* ; lower left: *No. 4*.
*Lent by Yale University Art Gallery, Collection of the
Société Anonyme*

161. Study for *The Jockey*, No. 5. 1921
Pencil, pen and black and red ink. 15 1/2 x 21 3/4 in.
Lower left in pencil: *Jacques Villon / No. 5*.
*Lent by Yale University Art Gallery, Collection of the
Société Anonyme*

162. Study for *The Jockey*, No. 6. 1921
Pencil. 5 1/2 x 14 1/4 in.
Lower right in pencil: *Jacques Villon* ; lower left: *No. 6*.
*Lent by Yale University Art Gallery, Collection of the
Société Anonyme*

*163. Study for *The Jockey*, No. 7. 1921
Pencil, pen and black ink on tracing paper.
10 5/8 x 17 3/4 in.
Lower right in pencil: *Jacques Villon / No. 7.*
Lent by Yale University Art Gallery, Collection of the Société Anonyme

164. Study for *The Jockey*, No. 8. 1921
Pencil, pen and blue and red ink. 11 1/4 x 18 7/8 in.
Lower right in pencil: *Jacques Villon*; lower left: *No. 8.*
Lent by Yale University Art Gallery, Collection of the Société Anonyme

*165. Outsider. 1921   (Color Plate III)
Pencil and water color. 5 7/16 x 10 3/8 in.
Lower right in pencil: *Jacques Villon / 21.*
Lent by Galerie Louis Carré

166. Le Jockey. 1921
Pen and green wash over pencil on tracing paper. Squared.
6 1/4 x 15 in.
Lower right in pencil: *Jacques Villon 21.*
Lent by Galerie Louis Carré

167. The Horse
Water color and pencil. Squared. 4 1/8 x 10 3/8 in.
Lower left in pencil: *Jacques Villon.*
Lent by the Art Institute of Chicago, Frank B. Hubachek Collection

168. NOBLESSE. 1921
Water color and pencil. 10 9/16 x 8 1/4 in. (sheet).
Lower left in pencil: *Jacques Villon / 21.*
Lent by Galerie Louis Carré

See painting of 1920, collection Ragnar Mottzau, Oslo,
Illus. Galerie Charpentier 1961, cat. 10.

169. UN OISEAU. 1921
Water color and pencil. 5 x 8 in.
Lower right in pencil: *J. Villon / 21.*
Lent by Galerie Louis Carré

See painting *La cage de l'oiseau,* 1952, collection Baronne
Guy de Rothschild, Paris, illus. Vallier p. 94.

170. FIGURE PAR PLANS. 1921
Pen, pencil and water color on tracing paper. Squared.
10 1/2 x 7 5/8 in.
Lower right in ink over pencil: *Jacques Villon / 21.*
Lent by Galerie Louis Carré

*171. SEATED BOY. 1922
Pen and India ink. 10 5/8 x 8 1/4 in.
Lower right in pencil: *22 / Jacques Villon.*
Boston Public Library

Used for "L'Appel de la Vie" (les garçons), etching, 1938,
(A.&P. 319).

172. LES VINGT ANS FIERS. 1930
Pen and water color.
9 3/4 x 7 7/8 in. (Sight).
Lent by Art Institute of Chicago, Frank B. Hubachek Collection.

Related to cat. 75. (A.&P. 227).

*173. NATURE MORTE AU PERROQUET. 1932
Pen, red and India ink and pencil. 10 15/16 x 17 3/8 in.
Lower left in black ink: *Jacques Villon / 32.*
Lent by Peter Deitsch Gallery

Related to etchings (A.&P. 247[I] and 247[II]) cats. 77 and 78.

174. LE POETE. 1933
Pen and India ink on tracing paper. 9 7/8 x 7 5/8 in.
Lower left in ink: *Jacques Villon.*
Lent by Galerie Louis Carré
Same subject as etchings (A.&P. 254 and 255) cat. 80.
See also cat. 175. A third drawing, Art Institute of Chicago,
coll. Frank B. Hubachek.

*175. LE SAVANT. 1933
Pen and India ink. 12 1/4 x 8 1/4 in. (sheet).
Lower right in pencil: *Jacques Villon*; below *33.*
Boston Public Library

See cats. 80 and 174.

175. LE SAVANT. 1933. Pen and India ink

*176. NOTRE DAME DE VIE. 1934
       Pencil. 7 1/4 x 10 5/16 in.
       Lower right: *Jacques Villon 34.*
       Lent by Art Institute of Chicago, John H. Wrenn Collection.

       Study for etching (A.&P. 263), cat. 81.

177.   ORPHEE (or Disjuncta Membra). 1934
       Pen and India ink on tracing paper. 11 1/8 x 12 1/2 in.
       Lower right in pen: *Jacques Villon / 34.*
       Lent by Galerie Louis Carré

       A painting, *Disjuncta Membra*, dated 1956 in coll.
       Svensk-Franska Konstgalleriet, Stockholm, illus. Oslo cat.
       1959, no. 68.

*178. STUDY FOR LE GRAND DESSINATEUR (Self-Portrait).
       1934
       Pen, India·ink and pencil on tracing paper. 10 1/8 x 9 1/8 in.
       Lower right in pencil: *Jacques Villon / 34.*
       Lent by Galerie Louis Carré

       See etching (A.&P. 266), cat. 82. A painting, 1935, coll.
       Mr. and Mrs. F. Steegmuller, illus. Vallier, p. 65; another,
       also 1935, Galerie Louis Carré, illus. Lassaigne 1950,
       pl. XV.

*179. STUDY FOR LE PETIT DESSINATEUR (Self-Portrait). 1935
       Pen and India ink on tracing paper; squared in pencil.
       6 5/8 x 5 3/8 in.
       Lower left in pencil: *Jacques Villon 35.*
       Lent by Galerie Louis Carré

       See painting cat. 190 and etching (A.&P. 267) cat. 83.

180.   COUR DE FERME CANY SUR THERAIN. ca. 1935
       Pen and India ink. 6 7/16 x 9 13/16 in.
       At left in pencil: *Jacques Villon.*
       Boston Public Library

       Study for lithograph, 1935, (A.&P. 437).

*181. LE JOUEUR DE FLAGEOLET. ca. 1938 / 39 (?)
       Pen and India ink. 10 9/16 x 8 1/4 in. (sheet)
       Lower right in pen over pencil: *Jacques Villon.*
       Former coll.: Oscar Stern, Stockholm.
       Lent by Mr. and Mrs. Irving M. Sobin

Related to etching 1938, (A.&P. 314), cat. 91; also painting
of 1939, illus. Vallier page 71.
Said to be a pupil of Villon seated in the artist's own
rocking chair, playing the recorder.

182.   MICHEL M. (Michel Mare, architect). 1940
       Pen and India ink. 19 x 12 1/4 in.
       Lower right: *Jacques Villon / 40.*
       Lent by Galerie Louis Carré

       Used for lithograph (A.&P. 445).

183.   LES ROIS MAGES. 1946
       Pen and India ink on tracing paper. 9 7/8 x 8 3/4 in.
       Lower left in pen: *Jacques Villon / 46*; below in pencil:
       à la memoire de Mary / Les Rois Mages.
       *Lent by the Art Institute of Chicago, Frank B. Hubachek
       Collection*

       See cat. 184.

*184. LES ROIS MAGES. 1947
       Pen and India ink. 10 1/2 x 8 in.
       Lower right in pen: *Jacques Villon / 47.*
       *Lent by Fogg Art Museum, Harvard University,
       Gift of Meta and Paul J. Sachs*

184. LES ROIS MAGES. 1947. Pen and India ink

186. MARCEL DUCHAMP. 1953. Pen and India ink

Study for etching (A.&P. 372) in Frénaud, *Poèmes de Brandebourg*, Paris, 1947, cat. 129.
Here the Magi are seen from behind. In the etching Villon returned to the front view as in preceding drawing, cat. 183.

*185. L'HOMME EN COLERE. 1952
Pen, India ink and pencil. Squared. 12 1/8 x 8 7/8 in.
Lower left in pen: *Jacques Villon*; in pencil: *52*.
Lent by Galerie Louis Carré

See etching, cat. 113.

*186. MARCEL DUCHAMP. 1953
India ink. 12 1/4 x 9 7/16 in.
Lower left: *Jacques Villon*.
Lent by Mr. and Mrs. Joseph M. Edinburg

Transfer drawing for etching, cat. 115.
See painting 1951, coll. Sonia Henie-Niels Onstad, illus. Galerie Charpentier, 1961.

*187. STUDY FOR PORTRAIT DE P . . . (Joseph Pulitzer, Jr.). 1954
Pen and India ink. 14 1/16 x 10 1/8 in.
Lower right: *Jacques Villon / 1954*.
Lent by Galerie Louis Carré

Study for painting of 1955, *Collection of Louise and Joseph Pulitzer, Jr.* (1957) cat. 70, fig. 43.

*188. LA FERME AU PIGEONNIER. 1954
Pencil and India ink. Squared. 16 1/4 x 12 3/8 in.
Lower right in pencil: *Jacques Villon / 54*.
Lent by Galerie Louis Carré

See *Le Pigeonnier Normand*, painting, 1953, illus. Charpentier cat. 1961 and two other paintings of same date, *La Ferme Normande*, coll. Louis Carré, illus. Vallier p. 96 and *Clos Normand*, coll. City Art Museum, St. Louis, illus. Vallier, p. 97.

185. L'HOMME EN COLERE. 1952. Pen and India ink

187. STUDY FOR PORTRAIT DE P (Joseph Pulitzer, Jr.). 1954. Pen and India ink

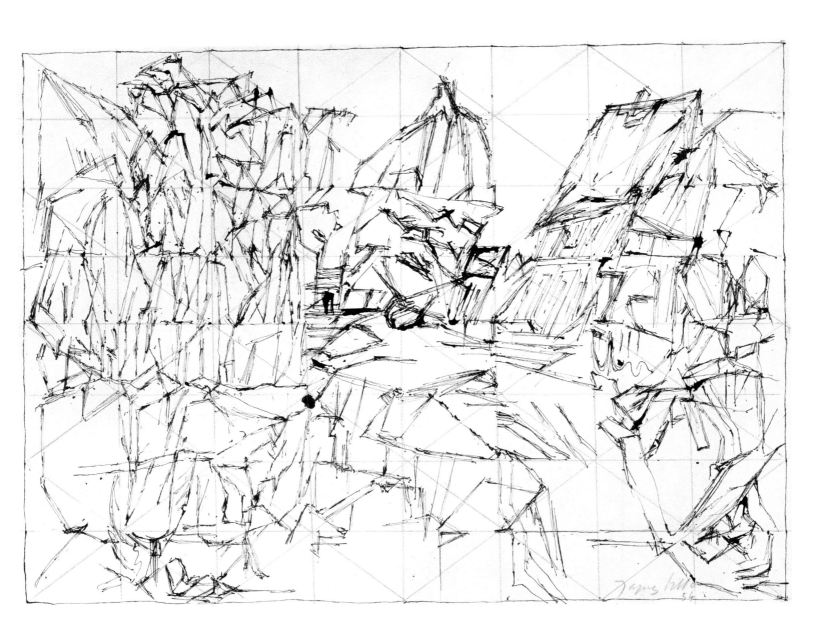

188. LA FERME AU PIGEONNIER. 1954. Pencil and India ink

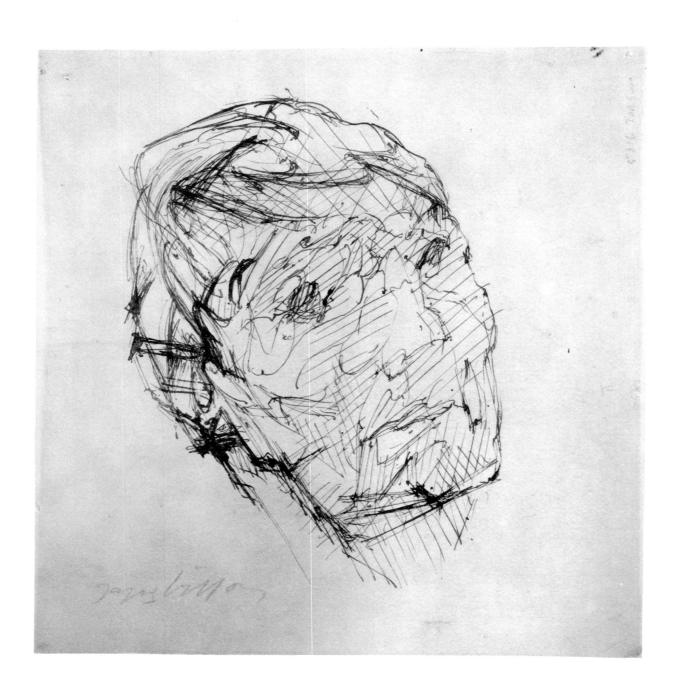

189. HEAD OF OLD MAN. Pen

189. HEAD OF OLD MAN.
      Pen and black ink on tracing paper.
      6 1/4 x 5 3/4 in. (Sight.)
      Lower left in pencil: *Jacques Villon.*
      Lent by Art Institute of Chicago, Frank B. Hubachek
      Collection

painting

*190. HOMME DESSINANT (Self-Portrait). 1935 (Frontispiece)
       Oil on canvas. 45 11/16 x 31 7/8 in.
       At left: *Jacques Villon.*
       Lent by Louis Carré

       See etching cat. 83 and drawing cat. 179.

sculpture   RAYMOND DUCHAMP–VILLON (1876–1918)

*191. PORTRAIT DE BAUDELAIRE. 1911
       Terra cotta. H. 15 in.
       Coll.: Mrs. Andrée Roosevelt
       Lent by Farnsworth Museum, Wellesley College

       See etching (A.&P. 204), cat. 60; drawing, cat. 154.